Challenge of the Marathon
A Runner's Guide

By the same author

Cross Country and Road Running

Challenge
of the Marathon
A Runner's Guide

Cliff Temple

Photography by Mark Shearman

Stanley Paul
London Melbourne Sydney Auckland Johannesburg

Stanley Paul & Co. Ltd

An imprint of the Hutchinson Publishing Group
17–21 Conway Street, London W1P 6JD

Hutchinson Publishing Group (Australia) Pty Ltd
PO Box 496, 16–22 Church Street, Hawthorne, Melbourne,
Victoria 3122

Hutchinson Group (NZ) Ltd
32–34 View Road, PO Box 40-086, Glenfield, Auckland 10

Hutchinson Group (SA) Pty Ltd
PO Box 337, Bergvlei 2012, South Africa

First published 1981
Reprinted 1981, 1982, 1984

Set in Linotype VIP Baskerville by
D. P. Media Limited, Hitchin, Hertfordshire

Printed and bound in Great Britain by
Anchor Brendon Ltd, Tiptree, Essex

ISBN 0 09 146431 5

Contents

About the Author

Cliff Temple saw his first marathon when he was one year old. It was the 1948 Olympic race in his former home town of Wembley and, perhaps inspired by that early insight, he became immersed in the athletics world very early on. He organized athletics meetings for his schoolfriends at the age of eight, and by thirteen had joined Thames Valley Harriers. Twenty years of dedicated training turned him from a slow thirteen-year-old, he says, 'into a slow thirty-three-year-old'.

Which means he is better known as a coach, journalist and author, the three channels through which he has sought to pass on to others his infatuation with, and enthusiasm for, the world of running.

As a coach, his own group of athletes includes international representatives on track, road and cross country. As a journalist he has been Athletics Correspondent of the *Sunday Times* since 1969, covering three Olympic Games, as well as contributing to athletics publications all over the world. He is a former Chairman of the British Athletics Writers Association.

As an author, his most recent book, *Cross Country and Road Running*, was a best-selling forerunner to *Challenge of the Marathon*.

Despite travel on athletics duty to dozens of countries around the globe, he is seldom happier than when running in the country lanes and footpaths around the ancient Cinque Port town of Hythe, on the Kent coast, where he now lives with his wife Clare, herself a former county runner, and their three children.

Acknowledgements

The author extends his thanks to the following, who were among those *Sunday Times* readers who followed his training advice, and survived to tell the tale: Richard Baker (Sheffield), Steve Barnes (Bristol), Bill Crotty (Uckfield), Andrew Dean (Totnes), Mike Ellacott (Letchworth), Simon Fermor (Putney), Bob Fever (South Croydon), Roger Garrington (Sunderland), Chris Gibbs (Nutfield), Mike Griffiths (Niederglatt, Switzerland), Geoff Hayles (Brighton), Ken Laidler (Tring), Peter McGough (Nottingham), John Milward (Wilhamstead), Ronald Peck (Birmingham), Andrew Puddicombe (Gosport), Eric Schofield (Tunbridge Wells), Barry Scott (Belfast), Roger Ward (Crediton), John Whelan (Liverpool), and David Wilson (Dorchester).

Thanks also to John Jewell, Past President of the Road Runners Club.

Author's note: Several short relevant passages which first appeared in *Cross Country and Road Running* have been revised and expanded for inclusion in this book. The Prologue first appeared in the *Sunday Times* in June 1978.

Prologue

'Whatever you do, don't drop out,' an athlete destined to be a winner tells me before the start. He can see I am definitely a loser. 'If you do, you'll regret it for months afterwards. And you'll still have to go through it all again another day.'

There are more than 250 of us, a record entry, lining up for the start in the private grounds of Windsor Castle. This year the traditional Goldenlay Polytechnic Harriers Marathon also includes the inaugural women's race: I look round the faces for one in particular, but she hasn't entered.

Several hundred yards after the start we pour through the George IV gates, which are fortunately open, and pass a large group of spectators who stand beside the ironically named Long Walk wearing that kind of pitying expression adopted when someone says: 'Well, I suppose you know what you're doing'.

At 300 yards I spot my wife, who is obviously confident that I will at least get that far. She is poised with the camera, ready to take a last photograph, but looking the wrong way. When she spots me, she panics and takes a colour picture of her left foot instead. 'Okay,' a runner beside me calls out. 'We'll all have to go back and start again.'

At 7 miles, the first refreshment station. It looks easy in the Olympic films: take a quick drink from the plastic cup on the run, then toss it down. What you actually do is to snatch a cup from the table; then the orange squash sloshes over the sides and sticks your fingers together, and if you try to drink while running, you end up spilling it up your nose and down your chest.

So for weeks I have been practising on training runs: my wife standing beside the road, holding a squirty plastic bottle, and myself attempting to grab it and propel a jet of liquid in the vague direction of my mouth, which I would simultaneously try to remember to open. Coordination was never my strong point, but eventually it works. So for four of the refreshment stations we label squirting bottles with my race number, 187, and hand them in before the start.

As you approach each station, a strategically placed advance official shouts out to other officials manning the drinks table: 'One hundred and eighty-seven!'. This gives the others time to sort through the labelled bottles and then, as you arrive panting in front of them, to shout back to the first official: 'Pardon?'

So this is the marathon, 26 miles and 385 yards. 16 miles gone, legs not too bad, breathing okay. But there is a long way to go. The mind wanders as we pass through leafy lanes, the nose twitches at the smell of cut grass. Wearing two big number cards, front and back, I feel like one of those playing cards in *Alice in Wonderland*. The numbers are big partly because they carry the names of both the race sponsor and the organizers. Goldenlay Poly? It sounds like a particularly randy parrot. I come up behind a runner whose own number is hanging down from his back by one pin, flapping up and down like a single wing.

'These numbers are a problem, aren't they?' I say in a spirit of that camaraderie which grows richer as the race progresses. If I had been sitting opposite him on a train, I wouldn't have dreamt of speaking. I tear it off for him like a Good Samaritan, and continue on my way, wondering if I ought to report him for not wearing a race number on his back. If I can help somebody. . .

Between 6 and 19 miles, I have actually been overtaking a few of the runners who started too fast. I have no thoughts of the dreaded 'Wall', which is supposed to hit you in the closing stages. But suddenly I realize that the runner in front, a greying man in a purple vest, who is apparently only shambling along, is not getting any nearer to me. I am going at the same pace. I do eventually catch him, talk to him, pass him, am passed by him, and make a bid to get away from him in the last mile. Only to be overtaken again in the final half-mile, as he finishes ahead of me. So at around 19 miles, we must both have hit that 'Wall'.

Looking back, I don't quite know what I expected to happen at that point, when the glycogen reserves run out. Was it a symbolic sheet of tissue paper stretched across the road, a flash of lightning, or a road-sign showing a pile of bricks? I noticed none of these things. I just became slower in return for more effort.

Our tour of the Berkshire lanes is over. We return to suburban Windsor. And at 24 miles I walk briefly for the first time, to ensure taking in some liquid at the last refreshment station. The last mile seems to take an age, and is not helped when, three-quarters of a mile from the end, a well-meaning spectator says, 'Come on, only a mile to go.'

We come into the finish area at the Windsor, Slough and Eton Athletic Club track. Seven hundred yards to run. There are spectators, applause and the drone of a loudspeaker. It is a scene with which I am familiar, having seen dozens of marathons. The clubmen are finishing; down the field, but finishing. These men on the track with me are the ones I have watched before, more often than the stars who can break 2 hours 20 minutes at the drop of a hat. Why do they do it? They're never going to win anything, are they?

But as I cross the line, feeling a sense of relief, emotion, and for a few seconds, the most intense kind of insularity, perhaps I know why they do it. I walk on, then slowly lie down on the grass. My time is 2 hours 52 minutes 27 seconds – over half-an-hour behind the winner, but who cares? A friend comes over, picks up my hand, shakes it and lays it down on the ground again. At that moment, I am not sure if I am still attached to it. The tiredness in my legs, though, is a wonderful feeling. I have run a marathon. Okay, so it's been done before. But not by me.

1

Winning Isn't Everything

Whatever other possibly unattractive aspects I may hereinafter mention about the tantalizing, glorious, strength-sapping challenge called the marathon, I must make clear from the outset my belief that in sport, perhaps even in life itself, it is actually the fairest event of all in terms of pure give and take.

Respect the marathon, be fair to it, and it will be fair to you. It will allow you to experience from running its demanding course a sense of physical achievement you will never forget, nor want to. Treat it too lightly, however, and underestimate the surreptitiously fatiguing effects of those 26 miles, and that long, silent ribbon of tarmacadam will suck you towards it, like the Devil's vacuum, long before the end.

Don't be put off. Completing the distance doesn't need magic potions or anything other than a progressive build up of steady running over a sustained period, starting and finishing at your own doorstep. I know. Even I've done it, and I'm probably the slowest, least skilful, most unco-ordinated physical specimen you're likely to come across outside a cemetery; two left hands, two right feet. So for me the appeal of long distance running events like the marathon is simply everything about it.

For it does not need the technical expertise of the discus thrower, nor the blazing inborn speed of the sprinter. A push, or a bad tactical position, will scarcely ruin your chance of success. You will not be let down by teammates, like a soccer player who has the game of his life and whose side still loses 14–1, or the opening batsman who ends the innings Not Out 3. Orienteering may be fun too, but the only time I tried it I couldn't even find my way to the Start, let alone to the controls.

Ideally for someone like myself, the marathon runner does not need a strong competitive spirit either, because only a small percentage of any marathon field, big or small, will actually be racing other runners. Most are more intent on simply pacing themselves most economically over the whole distance. Survival, in fact.

Long-distance runners don't have to be socialites, or gregarious extroverts in order to achieve success. It probably helps to be the opposite; fewer temptations or distractions! It doesn't matter who you know. It doesn't matter how much you have in the piggy bank. Neither influential friends nor a zillion pounds can help you one iota when those 26 miles stretch out in front of you.

All that counts is the training you have done in preparation to meet the distance. Thank God for a challenge which does not rely on a judge's opinion, like diving or ice skating. For me, invisible to barmen and waiters, that would be disastrous. ('Temple? Did you see him?' – 'No, I must have missed him too.')

Yet a private can beat a field-marshal in the Army marathon championship (as long as he remembers to salute as he passes him, presumably). And if a king beat everyone else in a marathon it would only be because he had been training hard for it, not because he was a king. No-one else can give you a leg up, but then no-one else can spoil it for you either. You don't have to wait, like a professional boxer, for your manager to agree terms, or for your title chance to come up. You don't have to live in hope of being spotted by a soccer talent scout on a bleak December Sunday morning match in the local park. More likely, you're running round the park. And then if, at the end of a marathon, you have not achieved what you set out to achieve, you cannot blame it on a bum decision, political bias, or blatant cheating by everyone else. You simply didn't run fast enough, or far enough, in training; not this time, anyway.

Not everyone who starts running later in life will achieve the success of men like Jack Foster, who emigrated from Liverpool to New Zealand at the age of twenty-four. By thirty-two this former cyclist was the overweight father of four children. As he tells in his book *Tale of the Ancient Marathoner*:

'One day I had the bright idea that I'd have a run for a while. It was summer time and the good weather inspired me. We were out for a picnic and a swim. I set off before lunch, thinking I'd have a run, then a swim. What I thought to be many miles later, I arrived back at the car.

' "What's wrong, have you forgotten something?" my wife asked.

'I didn't understand.

' "You've only been gone seven minutes," she said.

'Impossible. I was sure I'd run at least six or seven miles. I was soaked in perspiration and felt tired. I'd thought I wasn't in too bad shape physically. Not really overweight, though heavier than when I was riding the bike regularly. Now I was worried. If I was like this at thirty-two, how would I be when I was forty, or worse still fifty? So I began running – or jogging as I realize it was now.'

Nine years later, at the age of forty-one, he was the silver medallist in the 1974 Commonwealth Games marathon at Christchurch with a time of 2 hours 11 minutes 19 seconds, which put him among the ten fastest marathon runners of all time. And in 1978, at forty-six, he finished sixth of the 11,000 starters in the New York Marathon in 2 hours 17 minutes 29 seconds, in 80 degrees of heat. A runner literally half his age finished just 35 seconds in front of him. 'Perhaps what I've achieved as a runner may have inspired some other thirty-five-plus men to get up and have a go. I'd like to think so,' he says.

But Foster is a youngster compared to American Ivor Welch, who claims to be the world's oldest marathoner, and ran 5 hours 57 minutes in 1980 at the age of eighty-five! The same year another American great-grandmother, Ida Mintz, became the oldest woman to complete a marathon with 4 hours 45 minutes in Chicago at the age of seventy-four. In Britain, seventy-eight-year-old great-grandfather Bob Wiseman covered the London Marathon in 6 hours 16 minutes, while sprightly sixty-four-year-old Madge Sharples ran it in 5 hours 38 minutes 55 seconds with a broad grin on her face all the way, and said at the finish that she felt 'tremendous!'

Women have become more and more involved in marathon running, and the inclusion of the women's event in the 1984 Olympic Games will certainly not lessen its appeal. But whereas before the pattern for female runners in Britain was that hundreds and hundreds would start as twelve or thirteen year olds, then many would drop out of the sport again in mid or late teens (often purely for social reasons), now more and more mature women – often married, with young families – are starting to run with no dreams of Olympic glory. Instead it is simply for the opportunity it offers to break away from the nappies-cooking-laundry-shopping routine which might otherwise engulf their lives completely.

It might start simply as jogging for weight-loss as an alternative to those endless women's magazine 'new' diets. But it could develop into an ambition to run a marathon, however long it takes, by using an hour of the day when a woman's husband is at work, and the children are at school, to go out and run for fun. It's a perfectly feasible sports target: one of the very few, I would suggest, open to the busy housewife without totally disrupting her daily routine.

As we shall see, sports physiologists can find little but good health resulting from running for women, and former National cross country champion Ann Ford ran every day up to, and including, the day she had her first baby. Linda Schreiber, a New York housewife ('I was the classic non-athlete – twenty-five years old before I even rode a bicycle') started running in September 1974 on impulse, after a hectic day looking after her five children, who included eighteen-month-old quads. 'I loved my family and I knew all the household chores were practical and essential, but I often felt overwhelmed by my life,' she says. 'I knew I needed space and time of my own, and running was giving me that. Running gave me confidence, a particular ease. No matter what happened during the day, I felt I could handle it. My runs went from 3 to 5 to 7 miles over a two-year period, and now I generally run from 10 to 12 miles a day.' At the 1978 New York City Marathon she finished 11th of the 1100 women in the field, in a time of 2 hours 54 minutes 3 seconds.

In the USA, examples like that of Linda Schreiber have encouraged thousands of other women to start running. Each May a 10,000 metres (just over six miles) road race exclusively for women is held in New York's Central Park, attracting well over 4000 runners of all standards, from the incomparable world record-breaking Norwegian Grete Waitz to the slowest jogger. And Linda Schreiber herself has became nationally known by the title of her own book '*Marathon Mom*'.

If that sounds a little bit too yukky, then nearer home there is the equally inspiring example of Alison Blake from Plymouth. She started running in 1972, at the age of twenty-two and already the mother of four children, and in 1980 set a course record of 2 hours 50 minutes 45 seconds for the Duchy of Cornwall Marathon, from Land's End to Redruth, one of the toughest, hilliest races in Britain.

And of course Joyce Smith, the forty-five-year-old mother of two daughters, attracted more attention than at any time during her twenty-year career as a track and cross country international when she became only the third woman to break 2½ hours for the marathon in the Gillette London Marathon in March 1981.

But not everyone can realistically aim for the dizzy heights. Some runners set their own targets, like Jay Helgerson, a twenty-four-year-old ex-marine from Missouri, who set out to become the first athlete to run a marathon every week for one year in 1979. He managed to do it, averaging 2 hours 57 minutes 5 seconds for the fifty-two consecutive events, although he had to travel to twenty-one states to find his races.

'I figured somebody would do it eventually, and so it might as well be me. The idea was appealing. It was unique. A little crazy. It was really simple the way the thing came about. Nothing profound, no mystical voice told me "Thou shalt do fifty-two in a year . . .".

'I mean, I don't look like a marathoner. I'm not gaunt and hungry-looking like some of these guys. And I'm not fast. My personal record is 2 hours 42 minutes. I'm just an average runner, and I thought people could identify with what I was doing.'

Then there is Roger Bourban, a thirty-four-year-old restaurant-owner from Los Angeles, who claims the title of the World's Fastest Waiter, and runs marathons dressed in full waiter regalia, balancing a full bottle of mineral water on a tray. In his self-imposed rules, he doesn't change hands the entire way (which makes your arm tired, even thinking about it), nor is the bottle glued to the tray. When he crosses the line, he drinks the water. At the 1982 London Marathon he covered the course in 2 hours 47 minutes 21 seconds, 20 minutes faster than his previous best time, and considerably faster than many runners who weren't carrying trays.

At the 1980 New York Marathon, a runner named Ernest Conner ran the entire distance backwards, completing it in 5 hours 18 minutes, and adding (over his shoulder, I presume), 'I'll never do *that* again!'

Also at New York a separate, and quite unofficial, race has developed to see who can be the last runner home. In 1980 Anthony Geremia, a New York engineer, 'achieved' it in 7 hours 47 minutes. The slowest finishers in the 1981 London Marathon took around 7 hours.

The marathon challenge can be accepted by everybody. In the

London race, fifty-year-old Dennis Moore from Teddington, who is blind, covered the distance in just outside 4 hours, running attached to his helper, Wally Scott. In some American races, like the Boston Marathon, there are separate official categories for contestants in wheelchairs.

The major international marathons, like the New York and London races, have been accused of being little more than circus events. Whether or not that is fair, the fact is that people like circuses; they come to watch, and perhaps some of those spectating will become sufficiently inspired to next year want to become part of that circus.

A circus needs its strong man, its glamour, its clowns and its spectacle. For the crowd along the route of such 'mass' marathons, there is the same excitement of the sawdust ring in waiting for the leading international runners, the quickest woman, the characters, like the waiter and his tray, the personalities, like the Jimmy Saviles, and the oldest runners, and the backwards runners, and the slowest runners.

Watching a marathon confined to just several hundred reasonable standard male runners, which has been the traditional pattern of the pursuit in Britain until recently, can still be fascinating enough for those of us deeply involved in the sport. But to the casual observer, it must be about as fascinating as watching paint dry. There is room for both types of races, of course. But everyone vividly remembers the day the circus came to town.

On the wall above my desk is a large colour poster of the start of the New York Marathon. It has two purposes. It covers a damp patch on the wall quite nicely, but more importantly it provides constant inspiration. For both carriageways of the shimmering, silver-grey Verrazano-Narrows Bridge, which connects the start on Staten Island with Brooklyn, are obliterated by two broad streams of humanity climbing the rise and disappearing into the horizon on the start of a journey which will leave them exhausted, blistered, and, for those who reach the finish in Central Park, fulfilled.

All over the world, similar scenes are taking place. In Paris, Stockholm, Oslo, Rome, Melbourne, Los Angeles, thousands and thousands of runners, joggers and even non-runners are lining up to tackle an event which has commanded the deepest respect of some of the world's greatest athletes for almost a century. Bus drivers, insurance clerks, students, bricklayers, housewives, and people from every other walk of life with no previous experience of running are being taken over by a personal compulsive urge to train for the marathon. (You wondered why you had to wait so long for a number 36 bus? Now you know.)

As you look at the poster of that New York start, you can pick out the individual anonymous heads. Every one of that multitude must have been deeply motivated to be on that starting line in the first place, but no-one will ever know the full total of physical, mental, social and environmental difficulties which these runners collectively had to overcome along the way to be in a position even to face the 26 miles 385 yards with that mixture of fear and anticipation which pervades every marathon starting line. But perhaps all that is certain is that for every single one of those 15,000 runners in the race, there was at least one other somewhere in the world desperately disappointed because his or her entry for the same event had been rejected.

It would be the same deep sense of disappointment and rejection felt by those whose entries for the inaugural London Marathon were returned. A frustration that they would not be permitted to share what would be a real occasion as much as a pure running event. But then suddenly the marathon has become a victim of its own success.

The curiosity as to why such a hard test of physical endurance and mental tenacity should become so attractive to the British in the eighties is a topic for future generations of sociologists. It could provide material for a book in itself, and still not reach a specific conclusion. But there were 16,350 starters in the 1982 London Marathon, and 16,350 unique sets of circumstances which caused them to line up at Greenwich in the first place. Very, very few of them were there to try to *win* the race. And that surely is the key.

2

The Fight to Finish

In the small hours of a summer Monday morning, a crowd of around 4000 are gathered outside an hotel in Stockholm, cheering and serenading the two slim young men who stand on the balcony. It is 1912, and the pair of them have just been carried shoulder high from a banquet at the Swedish capital's Olympic Stadium.

Their names are Kenneth McArthur and Chris Gitsham, and a few hours earlier they finished first and second for South Africa, overcoming the oppressive heat, in the Olympic marathon.

The warm night sky is illuminated with fireworks, honouring the winners, and the vivid reds and yellows briefly light up a room at the nearby Serafino Hospital, where the singing and applause for McArthur and Gitsham are clearly audible.

Unhearing, on a bed in the room lies a feverish twenty-one-year-old Portuguese runner named Francisco Lazaro, who lined up with his sixty-seven marathon rivals opposite the Royal Box in the Olympic Stadium at 1.45 p.m. the previous day. Like them, he passed a medical inspection, and even declared that the course looked much easier than those he was used to in Portugal, where he had three times been national champion.

But after 19 miles of the race, he crumpled in the unremitting heat and was rushed to the hospital. Now, news of his grave condition is kept quiet in view of the festivities taking place after the race.

Later that day, as a result of sunstroke and heart failure, young Lazaro dies. 'In his delirium,' an eye-witness says, 'he seemed still to be struggling in the marathon.'

Before we move on to the question of how best to prepare for the marathon, it is worth looking briefly back to see who was responsible for the invention of the wretched race in the first place. And, despite its aura and mystique, to reduce it clinically to what it is: simply a long road race, whose exact distance lies not in Greek history but within this century, and whose origins as a sporting event barely stretch into the last. Only the occasion it symbolizes goes much further back.

The race commemorates a run supposed to have been made by a Greek messenger named Pheidippides in 490 BC, from the village of Marathon, some 23½ miles north-east of Athens. The Athenians had defeated the Persians in a great battle there, and Pheidippides is said to have run all the way to Athens with the news; around the latter stages of a modern marathon, most competitors probably wish he had just sent a telegram instead.

However, on arrival in Athens, Pheidippides gasped out the news of the victory to the city elders, and then collapsed dead (at which point I always envisage the elders looking at each other and asking '*What* did he say?').

Something which tends to keep Pheidippides firmly in the area of legend rather than fact is that his run was not mentioned by historians until nearly 600 years after the battle, although a courier named Pheidippides is said to have run from Athens to Sparta, covering 120 miles in two days, to request military help *before* the battle.

One theory is that the Roman historian and storyteller Plutarch created Pheidippides' run from Marathon to Athens simply as a means of transferring his tale from the battlefield to the city, instead of resorting to whatever was the Roman equivalent of 'Meanwhile, back in Athens. . .' Another theory is that Pheidippides' run is not mentioned by contemporary Greek historians because he was a deserter.

Whatever the truth, and we shall never know, what is certain is that the distance from Marathon to Athens is not the classic 26 miles 385 yards (42,195 metres) which the race has become. As a sporting event, its roots are relatively recent, springing from the preparations which were being made by the Frenchman, Baron Pierre de Coubertin, for the staging of the first modern Olympic Games at Athens in 1896.

A friend of de Coubertin, named Michel Breal, who was an historian, linguist and professor at the Sorbonne, suggested to the organizing committee the inclusion of two athletics events in the Games which would particularly reflect the glories of Ancient Greece. One was the discus throw, and the other was an endurance run along the original route supposedly taken by Pheidippides from Marathon. Both ideas were accepted and the endurance race, the marathon, eventually provided the highlight of those inaugural Games when the Greek shepherd Spiridon Louis gave the host nation its first and only victory of the Olympics in 2 hours 58 minutes 50 seconds. Greek runners also took second and third places on a course which was just under 25 miles.

The marathon quickly became an integral part of the Olympic Games on courses around that distance. But not without incident. At the 1904 Olympics in St Louis, the first runner into the stadium was an American named Fred Lorz, who was subsequently disqualified when he admitted that he had dropped out of the race with leg cramp at 10 miles, and accepted a lift in a car, which had churned up clouds of dust from the unmade roads all over his rivals before ultimately breaking down at 22 miles. So Lorz apparently ran the last three miles to the stadium and pretended to be the winner, until the other runners arrived. He explained later that it had been meant as a joke, but his national federation took a dim view, and suspended him from competition.

A little-known sequel to the story is that the incident weighed so heavily on Lorz's conscience afterwards that he literally ran himself into the ground in winning the 1905 Boston Marathon as a form of redemption. His feet were blistered and bleeding, and he collided with his own bicycle attendant in his exhausted state at the finish, falling heavily.

The Boston Marathon, the world's oldest annual marathon, was established in 1897. Almost all of the US competitors at the 1896 Olympics had been members of the Boston Athletic Association, and upon returning home had urged the Association to stage a marathon in the city, as they had been so enthralled by it. The first Boston Marathon was less than 25 miles, and it was only when the Olympic Games came to London in 1908 that the first ever race over the now-standard distance of 26 miles 385 yards was held.

The London event was due to begin in Windsor and finish at the White City Stadium, Shepherd's Bush, in West London. The actual start was staged on the private lawns of Windsor Castle because the children of the Royal Family wanted to see the runners, and it was also decided that the race should end opposite the Royal Box in the Stadium, so that Queen Alexandra could see the finish clearly.

That 1908 Olympic event also became widely known as 'Dorando's Marathon'. A diminutive Italian pastrycook from Capri, Dorando Pietri, was the first runner into the White City Stadium, as a contemporary newspaper account relates:

With 75,000 people in the seats and nearly 25,000 more packed into every inch of standing room all round the enormous amphitheatre of the Olympic Stadium, with the Queen of England in the Royal Box, surrounded by many members of her own and other Royal families, a miserable little figure tottered in at the North-Eastern entrance of the stadium. For a moment, as the news of his approach drew nearer, there had been a muffled roar of anticipation that rolled from tier to tier of iron and concrete, and re-echoed across the vast expanse of turf in sullen waves of sound.

But there was a sudden hush, almost a strangled sob of overwrought suspense, in all those hundred thousand throats when that small, withered man fell forward on to the first visible yard of cinder track, dizzy with excitement, devastated by the utmost atrocities of fatigue, but indomitable still. It was the Italian, Dorando Pietri. What followed was the most poignant scene that has ever been witnessed. It might have been beneath the skies of the South that we were all watching the struggles of some wounded toreador.

The wretched man fell down, incapable of going on for the two hundred yards that alone separated him from the winning post opposite the Royal Box. He was lifted up, and fell again. He struggled pitifully along to within fifty yards of the finish and collapsed. At that moment another competitor was seen struggling through the entrance, and after a terrible effort the Italian rose up and hurled himself with the last fragment of expiring will-power past the post.

He was carried away on a stretcher. After some twenty minutes the doctor was able to announce that he was going on well. But his stupendous efforts had been thrown away. Even at the price of a gold medal and the victory of the marathon race such agonies were too dearly bought. But Dorando was not even to get that. The doctor's testimony that the Italian, after he had fallen the last time on the track, would have been utterly unable to move without assistance was sufficient to prove – when proof was asked for – that the rule had been broken which clearly sets forth: 'No attendant will be allowed on the track in the Stadium'.

So the race was awarded to the second man home, Johnny Hayes of the USA, but Dorando had been taken to the hearts of the British people. When, three days later, Queen Alexandra presented the Olympic medals to the winners (as was the custom then), there was a special award for him: a gold cup, accompanied by a card headed Buckingham Palace, and in the Queen's own handwriting:

For P. Dorando
in remembrance of the Marathon race,
from Windsor to the Stadium
from Queen Alexandra.

The entire awards ceremony was brought to a halt by the acclamation given to the tiny Italian as he walked forward, clutching his cloth cap, and with a sprig of the King's oakleaves in his lapel, to receive the cup. The official with the megaphone simply couldn't make himself heard.

Now Dorando remains, three-quarters of a century later, as one of the most famous Olympians of all. The following year he and Hayes, the eventual gold medallist, both turned professional as a marathon craze swept the USA, and in 1909 they were racing marathons involving 260 laps on an indoor track at Madison Square Garden!

The scenes of Dorando's collapse remain among the most famous in athletics history, and the opening ceremony of the 1974 European Athletics Championships, which were staged in Rome's Olympic Stadium, included a 're-creation' by Italian athletes and officials of that dramatic finish 66 years earlier.

The exact distance between the private lawns at Windsor and the Royal Box at White City was measured as 26 miles 385 yards, and although the 1912 and 1920 Olympic marathons were held over courses of slightly different length, from 1924 onwards the curious distance set in 1908 was adopted as the standard marathon length.

The ultimate irony came many years later, when the 1969 European Athletics Championships were held for the first time in Athens, and the marathon, along the classic route, had to include a detour of several miles in order to bring it up to the required standard length! Appropriately, in the circumstances, it was an Englishman, Ron Hill, who won that race.

While times for the marathon are always difficult to compare because of the varying terrain of different courses (not to mention the differing lengths of those earliest races) one of the most significant performances between the wars came from a man considered to be the first of the great Finnish distance runners, Hannes Kolehmainen. In the 1912 Olympics he had won gold medals in the 5000 metres, 10,000 metres and (now discontinued) cross country events.

A vegetarian in his earlier years, Kolehmainen had actually run his first marathon at the age of seventeen, before concentrating on track racing. But in 1920 he won the Olympic marathon, held that year over its longest-ever distance of 26 miles 990 yards, in 2 hours 32 minutes 36 seconds, which would be equivalent to around 2½ hours for the now-standard length.

Times improved along with training methods, as in every event, but in the marathon there was still the chance for the winner to come from practically anywhere, and from any background. The Argentinian, Juan Carlos Zabala, for instance, could scarcely have had a worse start in life after being abandoned by his parents as a baby. But he took up competitive running at the age of sixteen in 1927, and in 1932 at Los Angeles the foundling became the youngest-ever winner of the Olympic marathon title.

Always the marathon provided high drama. For few other moments in sport can ever match the emotional charge of the entry into the Olympic stadium by the marathon leader. All eyes are fixed on a narrow tunnel entrance, the track has been cleared in readiness, and the announcement is made that the leader is now approaching the stadium. Who will the first runner be? And will he come shambling on to the track with weak, rubber legs, like Dorando Pietri? Or will he stride strongly into the arena, with a confident wave, and be able to enjoy the luxury of those final yards knowing that he is going to win?

As a boy I lived in Wembley, and often on summer evenings or winter mornings I found myself drawn to run the two miles to Wembley Stadium, turning down the long, deserted Olympic Way which leads to the slope up to the gates of the giant stadium which was the venue of the 1948 Olympic Games. It has been the scene of many other great sporting events, like that epic 1966 World Cup soccer final between England and West Germany. But always I was aware that I was exactly retracing the steps of the Olympic marathon runners, and I tried to imagine what it must have been like that day – not for Delfo Cabrera, the Argentinian whose name is immortalized nearby on a special plaque as marathon winner, along with the other 1948 champions – but for the Belgian runner Etienne Gailly.

Gailly, who had escaped from occupied Belgium during the war and served in Britain as a lieutenant in the Belgian Parachute

Regiment, had led that Olympic race for so much of the way, around Mill Hill, Radlett, Elstree, Stanmore and Kingsbury, and up that slope to the stadium. He entered the arena in the lead, but barely moving at a shuffle, and Cabrera took the lead from him some 300 yards from the line. A few seconds later, Britain's Tom Richards came past to take the silver medal. Gailly (who was killed in a road accident in Brussels in 1971) held on for the bronze medal, and was carried out of the stadium on a stretcher, barely conscious. Cabrera's name is on the plaque outside, but Gailly is the man remembered.

By contrast, the 1952 Olympic title in Helsinki was won with great ease by the remarkable Czech, Emil Zatopek, who had already won the 5000 and 10,000 metres titles before lining up for his first-ever marathon.

Zatopek recalls now that his entire plan in what was, for him, unknown territory was based on following Britain's pre-race favourite Jim Peters ('I didn't want to follow a nobody'), and that he had checked Peters's number – 187 – beforehand. Then, just to be sure, he had gone up to the athlete wearing 187 at the start, extended his hand and said, 'Hello – I'm Zatopek.'

'Hello, I'm Jim Peters', replied 187. And then Zatopek knew that he had the right man in his sights.

Peters, who had set a world best of 2 hours 20 minutes 43 seconds the previous month, led the early stages of the race, but by the halfway mark Zatopek had joined him. The Czech looked across at Peters and asked, 'The pace? Is it fast enough?'

Already feeling the effects of his earlier exertions, but not wanting to show it, Peters answered, 'The pace is too slow.' A few minutes later Zatopek put in a burst which took him clear of the Englishman, who eventually dropped out at 20 miles. Zatopek went on to win by 2½ minutes in an Olympic record of 2 hours 23 minutes 4 seconds, while the defending champion, Cabrera of Argentina, ran 8 minutes faster than at Wembley and yet was placed only sixth.

The name of Jim Peters is so well known in connection with another race that he did not finish – the 1954 Empire Games marathon in Vancouver – that his enormous contribution to the progress of world marathon-running is sometimes overlooked. But the Essex runner had set new levels of training mileage in the early fifties, and his 1952 run of 2 hours 20 minutes 4 seconds had clipped no less than 5½ minutes off the previous world best. He improved it three more times, down to 2 hours 17 minutes 39 seconds in 1954, prior to his last race on that sweltering day.

Peters had always believed in pushing himself to the absolute limit, and although even he realized that the 80°-plus heat in Vancouver meant that record-breaking would be impossible that day, he still ran so hard in the conditions that by the time he reached the stadium, his legs were no longer capable of supporting him.

He fell on the cinder track, rose, staggered, and then fell again, and again. The crowd, who had earlier that afternoon thrilled to the 'Mile of the Century' between history's only two sub-4 minute milers at that time, Roger Bannister and John Landy, were now stunned, some almost hysterical, at the new drama before them. They were torn between admiration for this stubborn rag-doll figure, desperately trying to finish the race (oh, those 385 yards!), and a wish to save him from further suffering.

Peters later recalled falling only about three times. In fact, it was nearer a dozen, and alongside him a troupe of officials and athletes matched his every agonized step, willing him on, but none daring to touch him, mindful of the Dorando Pietri incident (the name Pietri, incidentally, is the Italian version of Peters).

Finally, Peters reached the apparent haven of the finishing line, and the English team's masseur Mick Mays grabbed him as he was about to fall again, and helped carry him off. He was rushed to the Shaughnessy War Veterans Hospital, where he was put into an oxygen tent and injected with considerable quantities of saline solution to counteract the effects of dehydration.

'Did I win?' he asked a nurse when he came round.

'You did very well,' she replied.

For he had not won. Instead, the finishing line for the marathon had been another 200 yards further round the track, rather than at the point where all the track races finished. He had not been disqualified for receiving assistance to finish, like Dorando. Tragically, he simply had not finished.

The race itself was eventually won by Scotland's Joe McGhee in 2 hours 39 minutes 36 seconds, as only six of the sixteen starters completed the course in the oven-like conditions. The irony was that McGhee was still some three miles behind Peters when the Englishman staggered into the stadium. Peters would theoretically have had time, had he only known, to have rested in a shaded part of the track, and walked the rest of the way.

As a result of his harrowing experience, Peters retired from competitive running, although he made a full and complete recovery from his collapse. And his run, like Dorando's nearly half a century before, did not go totally unrewarded. On Christmas Eve 1954, a parcel arrived at his home, bearing a Buckingham Palace postmark. Inside was an Empire Games gold medal, mounted on a base, which was inscribed:

This gold medal was given to HRH the Duke of
Edinburgh at Vancouver, and presented by him to
J. Peters
as a token of admiration for a most gallant
marathon runner

A decade later, two other British runners helped to take the world's best marathon time for the distance towards the 2 hours 10 minutes mark. Coventry draughtsman Brian Kilby ran a world best of 2 hours 14 minutes 43 seconds in 1963, a year after winning both the Commonwealth and European titles (within six weeks), but this record was taken by his own Coventry Godiva Harriers team-mate Basil Heatley in 1964, with a run of 2 hours 13 minutes 55 seconds from Windsor to Chiswick.

Heatley also finished second that year in the Tokyo Olympic Games marathon (Britain's fourth silver medallist in the event) but his world best was in turn broken by the winner, the brilliant Ethiopian Abebe Bikila. His performance of 2 hours 12 minutes 11 seconds put him more than 4 minutes ahead of Heatley, and never was there a more relaxed winner. He even went through a session of vigorous exercises on the infield after the race, before Heatley arrived, to show how fresh he was feeling. Even more remarkably, his performance came just six weeks after he had undergone an appendicectomy. Yet Bikila had recovered quickly enough to become the first man ever to retain the Olympic marathon title, having won (barefooted!) in Rome four years earlier.

His attempt to complete the hat-trick had seemed quite feasible, as the 1968 Games would be staged at 7000-feet high Mexico City, and Bikila was himself a high-altitude dweller. But the attempt ended when severe leg pains forced him to drop out of the race after 10 miles. The following year he was badly injured in a car crash, receiving spinal damage which paralysed him from the waist down, and he died in 1973 at the tragically early age of forty-one.

The first man to average under five minutes per mile for the full distance (a pace which equates to 2 hours 11 minutes 6 seconds) was Derek Clayton of Australia, who clocked 2 hours 9 minutes 36 seconds in 1967. Clayton, a native of Lancashire who emigrated to Australia in 1963, has completely the opposite build to the normally accepted world class marathon runner's light frame. He stands 6 feet 2 inches and weighs 11½ stones, and his heavy physique, together with his aggressive way of training – always hard, high quality and high quantity running – probably contributed to his frequent injury problems. These involved nine surgical operations altogether, and partly led to his competitive retirement in 1974, although he still runs regularly and maintains his racing weight.

Despite these injuries he apparently improved his world best to 2 hours 8 minutes 34 seconds at Antwerp in 1969, a performance which has been surrounded by controversy ever since. In England the meticulous Road Runners Club has never recognized the mark on the basis of lack of evidence of accurate course measurement, and in the USA the 'bible' of the sport, *Track and Field News*, dropped the performance after nearly twelve years from its world record lists in 1981 in the light of a new investigation by the Road Runners Club of America. No relevant documents from the Antwerp race now exist, but the conclusion was that the course may have been short by one kilometre, and that it was measured by a car, which is not acceptably accurate.

In his defence, Clayton points out that the second and third runners in the race did not set personal bests, that he had warned the organizers that he would be trying for a world best, and had been told that the course had been measured with a calibrated wheel. 'I'm as certain as I can be that my record is accurate,' he says. 'I never thought the record would last this long. Otherwise, I might have measured the course myself. I only wish it could be proved that it is accurate.' It will almost certainly remain an unresolved area of controversy, because no more evidence is likely to be produced one way or the other. Certainly, Clayton's ability to run a time of 2 hours 8 minutes 34 seconds is not really in question.

But if the Antwerp course *was* short, then two of Britain's greatest marathon runners of the seventies, Ron Hill and Ian Thompson, have been denied the chance of being acclaimed 'world's fastest marathoner'. Hill, the Lancashire textile chemist and more recently a highly successful running goods business-man, was the instigator of many marathon innovations during the peak of his competitive career. He ran 2 hours 9 minutes 28 seconds in winning the Commonwealth Games title at Edinburgh in 1970, to add to his European title of the year before, and only Clayton's controversial run in Antwerp was faster at that time.

Then, in January 1974, Luton's Ian Thompson leapfrogged over Hill on the ranking list to take the Commonwealth title at Christchurch, New Zealand, in 2 hours 9 minutes 12 seconds. Again, only Clayton's 'record' was faster.

The rise from obscurity of Ian Thompson, real comic book stuff, has inspired club-level runners all over the world for years afterwards. Never really excelling on the track or cross country, and describing himself only as a 'scrubber', Thompson, then twenty-four, ran his first-ever marathon at Harlow in October 1973, simply to help out his Luton United AC clubmates in the team race.

The race was also the selection event for England's Common-wealth Games team but, totally unexpectedly in the star-studded field, Thompson won the race in 2 hours 12 minutes 40 seconds, then the fastest marathon debut of all time. Even he couldn't believe it. He had never raced further than 10 miles, and was merely aiming for 2 hours 20 minutes.

But the story gets better. Four months later, he won that Commonwealth Games race in the second fastest time ever, and another eight months on, in the sticky heat of Rome, he ran right away from Europe's best to win the gold medal in the European championships by 1½ minutes in 2 hours 13 minutes 19 seconds.

All it then needed was for him to win Britain's first-ever Olympic marathon gold medal at Montreal in 1976 to complete the fantasy. 'All' it needed. But on a nightmare day at Rotherham in May 1976, suffering from leg cramp, he failed even to qualify for Britain's Olympic team, finishing seventh in the AAA Marathon, his first defeat at the distance in five races.

Yet runners like Thompson, who has since been a consistent international performer if never reaching those early heights again, help to keep alive the magic of the marathon. What he did in 1973 and 1974 was in many respects illogical. Yet as long as someone can still achieve the illogical, the unexpected and the unpredictable in the event from time to time, the fascination of the marathon will not fade, and there is hope for everybody.

The unexpected has been the life blood of the marathon's history. Like the time Scotland's Jim Alder led up to the stadium at the 1966 Commonwealth Games at Kingston, Jamaica, but could not find any markers to show him the entrance. He ended up running along a corridor and down a flight of steps before finally emerging on the track in the daylight to discover he was now only the second man on the track, as England's Bill Adcocks had taken a different route. But Alder, in his desperation, managed to close a 50-yard gap on Adcocks in the 300 yards before the finish, and win the race.

The unexpected. Like the time American Frank Shorter approached the Munich Olympic Stadium nearly two minutes ahead of the rest of the 1972 Olympic field. The eyes of 80,000 spectators inside turned in eager anticipation towards the tunnel, out of which emerged to great acclaim . . . a heavily-built West German student named Norbert Sudhaus, clad in the blue and orange colours of his club, who ran almost a full lap of the stadium before running off the track and revealing his 'joke' to embarrassed officials and security guards. It left Shorter (who was actually born in Munich) totally bewildered as he then entered the stadium to a baffling torrent of booing and whistling directed, he was later relieved to learn, not at him, but at the student who had stolen his thunder and fooled so many of the crowd.

The unexpected. Like the occasion, four years later, when a little-known East German named Waldemar Cierpinski won the same Olympic title in Montreal. But as he crossed the line after completing the requisite one circuit of the track, he noticed that the lap marker still showed '1'. So he kept on running, just to make sure, by which time defending champion Frank Shorter had come in for second place, completed the correct distance and stopped. It must have been the first time that an Olympic marathon gold medallist had found the silver medallist waiting for him on the finishing line!

But Cierpinski made no mistake four years later in Moscow, where he became the second man (after Bikila) to successfully defend the Olympic title.

The unexpected. Like the time that a totally unknown twenty-six-year-old Cuban-born New Yorker named Rosie Ruiz crossed the line as first woman to finish the 1980 Boston Marathon, recording 2 hours 31 minutes 56 seconds, which six months earlier would have been a world best. But there was something a little suspicious about Rosie . . . she certainly didn't look like a world-class runner, either in build or style. On a hot day, she was barely damp from her efforts. And no one actually remembered seeing her at any point of the course before 24 miles or so. Some spectators even claimed they saw her join in then. She protested her innocence, and that she had indeed run the full distance.

But a few days later, amid much speculation, she was officially disqualified as the winner, and the race awarded instead to Canada's Jacqueline Gareau. (Ms Ruiz still maintains she ran the whole way, but I watched that race at various points around the course, and I'm afraid I don't believe her either.)

The unexpected. Like the time at an earlier Boston Marathon, in 1967, which was then still for male runners only, when race official Jock Semple jumped off a following bus and tried to push one of the athletes off the road. He had just realized that, horror of horrors, the figure in a baggy, shapeless tracksuit was a *woman* who had gatecrashed the race. She had even obtained a race number by entering as 'K. Switzer'. The K stood for Kathrine.

However, Kathrine's boyfriend, a 15-stone hammer thrower, was jogging alongside her at the time, and he removed Mr Semple bodily from the road instead. So Kathrine finished the race, and she and the hammer-thrower later married. Then they divorced. Today she is the best of buddies with Boston official Jock Semple, and women are officially welcome to run in the Boston Marathon, and from 1984 in their own Olympic Games Marathon. Such is life.

Those early days of women in the marathon consisted entirely of female runners gatecrashing men's races, at the risk of incurring the wrath of their own officials, never mind the men's. But it was then the only way they had of demonstrating that they could run the distance too.

The first such incident is as old as the race itself: a Greek girl called Melpomene (named after the Greek muse, Tragedy) joined in the first Olympic marathon at Athens in 1896, finishing the course in 4½ hours.

A French girl, Marie-Louise Ledru, finished 38th in a men's marathon in 1918, and there is a record of a Violet Piercey, in 1926, covering the Windsor-to-Chiswick course in 3 hours 40 minutes 22 seconds. Women began gatecrashing men's marathons in the USA in 1963, while a Scottish girl, Dale Greig, set an unofficial world best of 3 hours 27 minutes 45 seconds on the Isle of Wight in 1964. An ambulance followed her all the way!

A Canadian, Roberta Bingay, joined in the 1966 Boston Marathon unofficially, and it was the following year that Kathrine Switzer managed to line up with a number and survive that little roadside scuffle.

Meanwhile, mounting physiological evidence pointed to the fact that a woman could run a marathon as efficiently, if not quite as quickly, as a man. In 1972, as the women's best fell below three hours, American women were allowed to run marathons officially. In 1973 West Germany became the first country to hold an official national women's marathon championship. And in 1975, the Women's AAA introduced experimental rules to allow British girls over the age of twenty-one to run the distance.

The 'experiments' proved a success, no one collapsed and in 1978 the Women's AAA introduced an official national championship at the distance. Back in the USA, at the New York City Marathon, twenty-six-year-old Grete Waitz, an Oslo schoolteacher and a classical Scandinavian blonde, who had already established herself in European track and cross country running, smashed the women's world best in her first marathon by running 2 hours 32 minutes 30 seconds. 'Who are you?' asked the American journalists. Over 1100 American women had entered that New York race, alongside 13,000 men, as the US running boom of the seventies continued unabated.

The same year, the world governing body of athletics, the International Amateur Athletic Federation (IAAF) approved the addition of a women's marathon to the programme of the 1982 European championships. The venue? Athens.

In 1979, Grete Waitz reduced the women's world best to 2 hours 27 minutes 33 seconds, again at New York, which would easily have won her the Olympic men's marathon gold medal in any Olympic race up to 1948. In 1980, same girl, same race: 2 hours 25 minutes 41 seconds. Grete was running times which would have seemed impossible for a woman three years earlier. Patti Catalano of the USA became the second girl to break 2½ hours, Watford's Joyce Smith – at the age of forty-three – became the third, and New Zealander Alison Roe the fourth.

Meanwhile, Professor Ludwig Prokop, an Austrian member of the International Olympic Committee's Medical Commission, reported to the IAAF on the subject of women's marathon running:

Contrary to the traditional opinion that the physical performing capacity of woman is limited and that she cannot be exposed to greater strain mainly with respect to her endurance, sports physiological research and experience show completely different results. Apart from the fact that her muscular strength is less, physical performing capacity of women with respect to endurance is absolutely, as well as relatively, equal to that of men. Under extreme conditions of constant performance, women must even be rated higher than men. This is explained by the fact that the female heart may be excellently trained just like that of a man.

According to examinations carried out in the USA, Czechoslovakia, Federal Republic of Germany and German Democratic Republic even in child age endurance performances only slightly differ between boys and girls aged between seven and thirteen years. Therefore, after equally long periods of training, women develop an oxygen absorption per kilogram of bodyweight nearly similar to that of men. Another decisive characteristic, which is probably sex-linked, is oxygen utilisation being more favourable in women than in men. This is also confirmed by the fact that women are at least as resistant or even more resistant to high altitudes than men; mountain sickness (hypobaropathy) is less common in women than in men.

Practical experience with women as long distance runners confirms performance physiological results. Although the marathon race for women has been carried out as a regular competition only for a few years and only by a few women, there are already about 30 women running the marathon under 2 hours 40 minutes, and a best performance of well under 2 hours 30 minutes has been achieved. So far no accidents have been observed during marathon races for women, so this is no argument against competition for women over longer distances. Experiences with long distance swimming for women are similar. In swimming as well as in running, women approach the performances of men as the distances increase, and going over extremely long distances they often achieve better results than men.

Professor Prokop concluded, 'There are no relevant sports medical grounds against marathon running for women.'

At their meeting in Los Angeles in February 1981, the International Olympic Committee decided that the case for women had been proved. At the 1984 Olympic Games in that city, eighty-eight years after Melpomene had gatecrashed that original marathon race in Athens, women would be allowed to compete in the Olympic Games over 26 miles 385 yards.

Among the top women runners, the news was acclaimed. But for the vast majority it would in practical terms really make very little difference. For during the 1970s in the USA the marathon had been taken over by the masses. It was no longer an event just for the dedicated 100-mile-a-week athlete; it was a challenge being explored with no qualms by a much wider circle of healthy adults – and even children.

Events like the New York City Marathon, which had begun with just 126 runners on a circuit within Central Park in 1970, mushroomed to become a giant international festival with a route through the city's five boroughs, and which virtually closed New York down for the day. In 1980, more than 30,000 had applied to run in the race, and half had to be turned down. Up and down the country on 1 June would-be entrants stood in queues at all-night post offices waiting for midnight so that they could post their entry applications with a 12.01 a.m. postmark, the earliest time applications would be considered.

Traditional events like the Boston Marathon, with its Centenary in sight, suddenly had to introduce strict time limits for entry in the early seventies to control the vast numbers wanting to pack the narrow roads from the start at the little town of Hopkinton along the 26 miles to Boston's Prudential Centre finishing line.

New marathon races blossomed, and there are now around 300 held annually in the USA. The shorter road races attracted even larger fields: in 1980 the 6-mile Peachtree Road Race in Atlanta, Georgia, had no less than 25,300 starters, while in San Francisco the 7½-mile Bay to Breakers race had 24,000.

In Britain the marathon boom, which was finally unleashed by the 1981 London Marathon, has been creeping up on us for years. Entries for all road races had been growing steadily if unspectacularly; new races had been springing up all over the country, including a rising number of non-competitive 'fun runs'. Sales of tracksuits and training shoes increased dramatically; the circulation of the athletics magazines grew.

One major cause for the boom, of course, was the growth of jogging in recent years. Increasing medical evidence that physical activity was beneficial for maintaining (or recapturing) good health, set thousands of people out on the roads, paths and canal banks of Britain simply jogging.

For some, though, despite the general feeling of well-being the activity engenders, often accompanied by a significant weight-loss and lowered pulse rate, there was still a nagging air of aimlessness about this type of exercise. After a time it seemed, literally, to go round in circles. For those getting fit after years of inactivity, it was the ideal, gently progressive way of doing so, of course. But once you were fit enough to run for half-an-hour, or an hour, what next? Maybe debauchery wasn't so bad after all. . .

To fill this void, the *Sunday Times* National Fun Run was launched in September 1978, in Hyde Park, and the instant response showed that there was a huge demand for some form of running event for those who did not want to take part in open competitive athletics, but still needed some motivation to keep on running. That first year there were 12,000 entries for the series of 2½-mile runs (not races) grouped by age and sex, and each year since then the entries have grown rapidly. Banks, factories, offices, pubs, service units and colleges have been among those entering teams with the only prizes being the gold, silver or bronze category-certificates awarded to every runner, whether a member of a team or not.

Such challenges as the marathon and the new wave of fun-running would inevitably hook up eventually like lines on a graph drawing inexorably closer. The question was simply, when would they meet? And while the 1981 London Marathon will certainly be looked upon as the most significant single day, with national attention focussed on it by saturation media coverage and superb BBC Television pictures, there were other significant events too.

The 'Masters and Maidens' Marathon, for instance, is not a race as such but 'a timed run over the marathon distance'. It is open to women, men over forty, and men aged twenty to forty who have not previously broken three hours for the distance. It is staged each October on a pleasant country route south-west of Guildford, and in 1980 attracted a record entry of over 900.

But its real significance lies in the fact that it was started back in 1975, long before the British marathon boom, and was really ahead of its time in giving those slower runners (or even those outside the official age limits) a chance to at least run the marathon distance in relaxed surroundings in the company of many others of similar standard.

It is organized by a group called the MABAC Fun Run League, who very sensibly also organize 'stepping stone' events at 10 miles in July and 15 miles in September for those preparing for the marathon itself. Sadly, its originator, Alan Blatchford, died shortly before the 1980 event, but his name will live on in the event's title.

In May 1980, five months before the London Marathon was even announced, the inaugural People's Marathon, organized by the Centurion Joggers in Chelmsley Wood, near Birmingham, reached its entry limit of 750 well before the day. Hundreds more had to be turned down, despite (or perhaps because of) its own restrictions to runners who had not previously attempted a marathon, or broken 2 hours 50 minutes since January the previous year.

With a planned and controlled expansion masterminded by its organizer, John Walker, over its first couple of years it quickly became another landmark event for the fun-runner. In 1981, 2000 ran. For years British marathons had imposed time limits to keep out the slower runners. Now there were events with time limits to keep out the *faster* runners. And the joggers and club runners of Britain flocked to them.

They have not attracted a fraction of the publicity of the London Marathon. But they were the real pioneer events, and their part in the marathon growth must never be underestimated.

In the USA, where the marathon boom was inspired more than anything else by Frank Shorter's Olympic marathon victory in 1972, there were never age restrictions. In Britain, you have to be eighteen to race a marathon under national association rules. Until recently, running a time outside 3½ or 4 hours would find the race officials packed up and gone home. At some races it still does. But there are now other events where, if you are prepared to spend seven hours on your marathon, the organizers are prepared to wait for you.

So we have at the moment in Britain something of a dichotomy: while many marathon organizers are glad to see the boom, there are others steeped in so-called 'pure' athletics, who are unwilling to accept that joggers in funny hats, sawn-off jeans, plimsolls and stereo-radio headphones, can possibly be seen as part of the same sport which has witnessed Jim Peters, Abebe Bikila, Ron Hill and Ian Thompson sweating and grafting their way to world recognition.

It is still outside their comprehension that there could even *be* individuals – voting, rate-paying, educated, married – whose sole aim is simply to run a marathon, however slow, without necessarily wanting to join an athletic club, or run other distances, or on the track. It is even seen as a form of sacrilege ('In my young day, we all turned out in the club one-mile championship, shot-putters, hammer-throwers, the lot. . .'). And there are those whose main worry about the running boom is whether or not all of these newly-converted runners are amateurs or not, as defined by the rule book. Yet if they really eliminated all the non-amateurs in athletics, we'd probably lose most of our Olympic team for a start!

Fortunately, this negative attitude is very much a minority view. If you have taken up running simply in the hope of one day completing a marathon, then among the athletes of Britain you will find nothing but encouragement and help in your aim. It is something of which the road-running fraternity have always been particularly proud.

But let us hope too that the new-found respectability and appeal of the event in Britain, and above all the much wider appreciaton of what it takes to run 26 miles 385 yards, will inspire, encourage and motivate those established runners to try even harder (if it is possible) to remedy one major shortcoming in British athletics. And that is that despite constantly bemoaning our lack of athletics facilities, we have managed to produce Olympic champions in recent years in events like the decathlon, the pentathlon, the long jump and the 400 metres hurdles. But never, ever, a gold medallist in the one event which needs no facilities at all: the marathon.

3

First Steps to 26 miles 385 yards: Training

So you want to be that first British athlete to win the Olympic marathon gold medal? Or perhaps you just want to run a marathon, and you think that, with training, you can do it. Or, more likely, you wonder *whether* you can do it. Because there is not a single athlete, from Olympic champion down, who can state with 100 per cent certainty at the start of any marathon race that he or she is definitely going to finish. There are too many unpredictable factors.

But are you ready to put in the months and months of regular training needed as the slimmest base from which you can realistically hope to run a marathon? Obviously, the better prepared you are, the more thorough your training background, and the greater your experience as a runner, the higher your chances of being able to run the full distance.

Also, the better marathon runner you become, the more other considerations, like competition and performance, will eventually become relevant to you. Sometimes a top-class marathon-runner drops out of a race, not because he is incapable of finishing the course at a slower rate, but simply because competitively it has not gone well. Or perhaps he realizes that the final time is going to be relatively poor, and he does not want to push himself into the most traumatic part of the race to suffer unnecessarily, and possibly delay his return to the fray another day.

Of course, there are also runners who refuse to quit, whatever the circumstances, however badly the race has gone, and who finish in shoes stained with blood from raw blisters, or with agonizing cramp, or limping with a muscle strain, when perhaps it would have been wiser to stop altogether.

That decision has always been very much a personal one, except in the case of imminent physical collapse. The Amateur Athletic Association Rules state: 'A competitor must at once retire from the race if ordered to do so by a member of the medical staff officially appointed.' Fortunately, this situation arises very rarely.

But for those of more modest ambition who wish to complete a marathon, stopping to walk when you feel the need (which does not automatically disqualify you, as some people think) is a wise move. In fact, you could theoretically walk the whole way if you wanted to, but that would seem a rather pointless, selfish exercise in what is after all a running event, and you would be taking a great chance on anybody still being at the finish line waiting for you.

So let us examine in the following pages, stage by stage, what you need to do and what you need to know in preparing for your first or your fiftieth marathon. Let us look at some training schedules which might suit you, whether or not you are already a runner, and let us hear as well from some of the runners who have already followed this type of schedule: their experiences, their successes – and their failures. We can learn from them all.

And let us listen also to some of the runners who for years have been among the best marathon performers in the world, and who know what it is like to run those 26 miles as fast as anyone has ever run.

The Effects of Training

Running is a simple process. Oxygen is inhaled, absorbed into the blood stream through the lungs, and carried by the blood to the muscles, thus enabling them to perform the activity required of them, which in this case is to run. That is a greatly simplified version of what actually happens, but the limitations on running are very much governed by the ability of the body to carry out the oxygenation process efficiently and continuously.

Through regular training, though, it is possible to increase that ability considerably and thus raise the level of athletic performance. For example, nearly 6 litres of air can be processed in a single breath by even an averagely trained distance runner, while an untrained person would probably manage less than 5 litres. A trained runner also has more red blood cells, and in each cell more haemoglobin (an iron-containing protein which provides the colour and bulk of the contents of the cells, and is responsible for the transport of oxygen) than an untrained person, and can thus absorb and move more oxygen from the lungs to the muscle tissues.

As a result of training, the heart, which is itself a muscle, enlarges and strengthens to the point where it can pump a much greater volume of blood with more efficiency. The runner's resting pulse rate becomes correspondingly slower the fitter he gets, as the heart needs to beat less often to move the same amount of blood at rest. An average healthy non-runner might have a resting pulse rate of 72–74 beats per minute whereas a well-trained runner may have a resting pulse rate of only 40, or even lower.

The training effect, achieved through regular running, is simply a form of adaptation made by the body to be able to cope with the work asked of it. The adaptation is a response to the stress imposed by running, and once a certain level of fitness is achieved, the 'stress' has to be increased by graduating the amount or intensity of training, to keep the body adapting to a higher degree of fitness.

All the time, the volume of air that can be taken in and processed through the lungs and the rate at which it happens, the oxygen-carrying capacity of the blood, and the ability of the circulatory system to transport oxygenated blood to the muscle tissues, are being greatly increased. Muscles become stronger and more efficient. Stamina increases. Body fat, which hinders the processes, is being burned up and reduced to a minimum. On every training run you are becoming a fitter, stronger, better-prepared athlete.

During a 20-mile run, for example, massive amounts of blood are moved around the body, the pulse is kept at a reasonably high and steady level (thus providing the type of stress to which the cardiovascular system will adapt and strengthen for the future), and greater capillarization occurs, allowing the blood more routes to get oxygen to the muscles.

In undertaking any training programme for the marathon, whether at beginner or advanced level, the single most important consideration is achieving regularity in training, on a graduated scale, to provide the necessary stress for adaptation and improvement. There are events, particularly the shorter middle-distance track events, which rely on a fair measure of that type of training (very fast, getting into an oxygen 'debt', and holding it) for their success. If you never rehearse the physical conditions produced by such a race, you cannot expect to be able to cope with them on the day.

And so it is with the marathon, in a more relaxed way, as you seek stamina, economy and efficiency in your running, built upon hundreds and hundreds of training miles.

The purpose of having any sort of training programme then, whether it is taken from this book, or one you devise yourself, is to allow you to follow a graduated path from *now* (when perhaps you can jog for only five minutes) to *then* (possibly eight months from now, when you hope to be able to run a marathon).

The training schedule is the map for your journey. When you are driving along a road, you cannot necessarily see your destination, but you know the map will get you there if you follow its directions. You may have to stop briefly to mend a puncture, or to get some petrol. But by and large if you keep going in the same direction, you'll reach the horizon.

All the training schedules in this book, whether for the new or experienced, are balanced. They are balanced from day to day, as well as week to week, because if you go out on a Saturday morning and complete the longest continuous run of your life, you are not likely to want to get up on Sunday morning and be faced with the prospect of having to go even further. Instead, you will need a shorter run, to consolidate, to work any stiffness out of your legs, and to be able to gloat over having achieved yesterday's run. Only later in the week do you run long again.

A simple rule of thumb for getting fitter is: Hard work plus rest equals success. Hard work, plus hard work, minus rest, equals injury.

The training schedules are divided into two sections. The first section, contained in this chapter, is meant primarily for joggers and newcomers to running, who want to build up towards a marathon from virtually no background or previous experience. The second section, in the next chapter, is aimed at those who are already fairly fit, perhaps club runners covering 40 miles a week or so, who would like to use their background and develop it towards a reasonable marathon. And this second section goes on to recommend the type of training schedule a top-class international marathon runner of the eighties might use.

A primary difference between these two sections is that the first deals in 'running minutes' while the second is confined to miles of running. Don't mix them up, or you may find yourself out on a Sunday morning 90-mile run!

The reason for the difference (which has intriguing possibilities if misused) is that from practical experience joggers and new-runners seem to prefer being set a specific time to run regardless of distance, because it is a unit with which they are familiar and which they can control. But more experienced runners will have a greater familiarity with miles, and in fact 'miles per week' is the currency club runners use, like motorists discussing their relative 'miles per gallon'.

We may be making a rod for our own backs by using two separate systems, especially as the jogger will eventually become a club runner. But by that time he or she should have more working knowledge of pace and distance.

There is another difference. The 'joggers/new-runners' schedules.graduate from the first day to the last (the marathon itself) with no hint of any other competitive or non-competitive events being included. This is because in my recent experience many of the new potential marathoners have eyes only for the day when they will be able to run that 26 miles 385 yards, and they are content to go out running every day with no thought or desire for any other, shorter type of running event, even if one is right on their doorstep.

For instance, I was advising one quite fit young man in his preparation for the London Marathon, and I kept suggesting various low-key running events in which he could take part as a 'mental break', and to see how he was faring. At first, he kept making excuses for each date I suggested, but finally he admitted that he really didn't want to take part in any other running events. All he wanted to do was to train for the marathon. And he was not, it transpired, alone in this attitude.

So the schedules show no intermediate events, not even the *Sunday Times* National Fun Run! But I nevertheless suggest that the potential marathoners do keep their eyes open for road races and fun runs in their area; anything that will give them even a little taste of competitive experience.

The schedules for the most experienced runners do indicate points at which a road race of 10–20 miles might be beneficially introduced to break up the grind of training. It still has to be accepted that if the marathon is the prime goal, then training cannot be eased down too much before the big day, and that some races will have to be undertaken (or missed out) in a state of slight residual fatigue. Occasionally, to make up the quota of miles for the week, it may even be necessary to train on the morning of one of these races, or afterwards.

But this has previously been an effective way of long distance preparation: to 'train through' lesser races.

Don't let anyone tell you that a distance runner is someone who shakes off germs like water off a duck's back, and is a constantly lively soul, bubbling with health and effervescence. No, a distance runner in training is someone who is perpetually tired, usually moving sluggishly from one comfortable perch to another. His approach is normally heralded by the sound of someone sniffing.

You run a long way, you get tired, you barely recover, and then you run a long way again. Consequently, you are more susceptible to any bugs floating around than the average person, and you are always one step away from an excruciating pain in your lower left leg, or a sharp twinge in your hamstring.

Distance runners getting together before a race to compare their latest injury symptoms can be like a gaggle of gossips. Everyone pretends to listen, but really they are just dying to get in with their own three ha'pence worth.

Sometimes as a distance runner you have just a little too much time to think to yourself, 'Is my left foot hurting today? Yes . . . yes, I think it is! And the right knee? . . . Yes, that too.' By the time you get home you're barely fit enough in your own mind to crawl upstairs and get somebody to call an ambulance. There are only three normal states of health for a serious distance runner: injured, recovering from injury, or deciding which injury you'd like to have next. Such is the paradox!

The Beginner's 52-Week Build-Up Programme

If I had to pick a figure, I would say that one year is the minimum amount of time a normal, healthy, unfit person should reasonably allow to prepare from scratch to run the marathon distance. And in that year he or she would have to run regularly six days a week at a comfortable pace for increasingly long periods of time, as indicated in running-minutes on the chart, which has been specially prepared for this book.

Having said that, I will doubtless be inundated with details of the hundreds of people who did so on much less. All I can say is: 'I know. But what I wrote was that one year is the minimum amount a normal, healthy, unfit person *should reasonably allow*.' A little later I'm even going to suggest how it could be achieved in less than half that time when you're really desperate, and we'll hear about people who did. But I still recommend that one year minimum.

What the bare columns of figures on pages 45–47 cannot tell you, as your eyes scan over the increasing denominations of running-minutes, is that running for 40 minutes after 14 weeks will not seem eight times harder than running for five minutes now. It will take eight times longer, certainly, but as your cardio-vascular fitness increases, so the longer runs may eventually seem actually easier than your first ones, as your lungs, heart and muscles respond to the slight stress to which you are subjecting them, and in turn become stronger and more efficient.

In that initial 5-minute session, we are not looking for 1¼ miles; instead, we are simply seeking 5 minutes of steady running, close to the pace at which you eventually hope to run the marathon. An average pace of 10 minutes per mile, for instance, will give you a final time of 4 hours 22 minutes 13 seconds; a 7½-minute mile pace would give you 3 hours 16 minutes 39 seconds and a 5-minute mile pace would end up as 2 hours 11 minutes 6 seconds. But that last figure would certainly be too ambitious!

It is as well to reserve one day as a rest day, so that you have a regular recovery space at the end of the week before tackling the weekend's running, which will normally entail a relatively high proportion of the week's total.

From Week 27 to Week 42, the chart shows two separate runs on the Saturday, as a subtle method of layering the overall increase. In fact, in marathon terms, one single run of 60 minutes could be said to be more beneficial than two of 30. But that is to overlook the mental lift of not having to run quite so far each time, and perhaps even faster, which could well outweigh any shortfall in conditioning. There are plenty of other long runs in the week, so enjoy the brevity. It changes again in Week 43, so why hurry?

The week is shown in its chart form from Sunday to Saturday, and its framework is built around the supposition that the runner has Saturday and Sunday as weekend. For those who haven't, or who work shifts, or have midweek days off, amend the days of the week at the top of the columns to suit you. But try to keep the progression of runs themselves intact.

It would be miraculous if you went through the whole year without missing a single scheduled session as a result of illness or injury. If you do have to interrupt the schedule, when you have recovered it is best to gradually pick it up at a point some days before you left off; don't try to pick it up where you otherwise should have been. You may then have to adjust the final weeks, but remember to taper right down before the race itself, as shown in Weeks 51 and 52.

Schedule No. 1 The Beginner's 52-Week Build-Up Programme

NB Values are in 'running-minutes'

	SUN	MON	TUES	WED	THUR	FRI	SAT
Week 1	5	5	8	5	8	5	8
Week 2	10	5	10	5	10	5	10
Week 3	12	8	10	8	12	5	12
Week 4	15	8	10	8	12	5	12
Week 5	18	8	12	8	12	8	15
Week 6	20	8	12	10	12	8	15
Week 7	20	10	12	10	15	Rest	15
Week 8	25	10	15	10	15	Rest	15
Week 9	25	10	15	10	15	Rest	20
Week 10	30	10	20	15	15	Rest	20
Week 11	30	15	20	15	15	Rest	20
Week 12	35	15	20	20	15	Rest	20
Week 13	35	20	20	20	20	Rest	25
Week 14	40	20	20	25	20	Rest	25
Week 15	40	20	25	25	20	Rest	25
Week 16	45	20	25	30	25	Rest	25
Week 17	45	25	25	30	25	Rest	30

Schedule No. 1 – contd.

	SUN	MON	TUES	WED	THUR	FRI	SAT
Week 18	50	25	25	30	25	Rest	30
Week 19	50	25	25	30	25	Rest	30
Week 20	55	25	20	35	25	Rest	30
Week 21	55	30	20	35	30	Rest	30
Week 22	60	30	20	35	30	Rest	30
Week 23	60	30	20	40	30	Rest	30
Week 24	60	30	25	40	30	Rest	30
Week 25	60	30	25	45	30	Rest	30
Week 26	65	30	25	45	30	Rest	30
Week 27	65	35	30	50	40	Rest	2×20
Week 28	70	35	30	50	40	Rest	2×20
Week 29	70	35	35	50	50	Rest	2×20
Week 30	75	35	35	50	50	Rest	2×20
Week 31	75	40	45	60	40	Rest	2×20
Week 32	80	40	45	60	40	Rest	2×20
Week 33	80	40	45	60	40	Rest	2×25
Week 34	85	40	45	60	40	Rest	2×25
Week 35	85	40	50	45	60	Rest	2×25
Week 36	90	40	50	45	60	Rest	2×25
Week 37	90	40	50	45	60	Rest	2×30
Week 38	95	40	50	45	60	Rest	2×30
Week 39	95	40	55	45	60	Rest	2×30

Schedule No. 1 – contd.

	SUN	MON	TUES	WED	THUR	FRI	SAT
Week 40	100	45	55	45	60	Rest	2×30
Week 41	100	45	55	45	70	Rest	2×30
Week 42	110	45	55	45	70	Rest	2×30
Week 43	110	45	60	45	70	Rest	60
Week 44	110	45	60	45	70	Rest	60
Week 45	120	45	60	45	75	Rest	60
Week 46	120	40	60	45	75	Rest	60
Week 47	130	40	70	45	80	Rest	60
Week 48	140	40	70	45	80	Rest	60
Week 49	140	40	75	40	70	Rest	60
Week 50	150	30	60	30	70	Rest	60
Week 51	120	20	40	30	60	Rest	40
Week 52	80	Rest	30	20	Rest	5	THE RACE

The Beginner's Sunday Times *21-Week Crash Programme*

When the date of the first London Marathon (29 March 1981) was announced in late October 1980, I spent some time working out a training schedule which would fit into the 21 weeks then remaining between those dates, and which might enable a potential participant to scramble together enough fitness to get round the course.

Then that schedule was published in the *Sunday Times* with the same advice as I'm going to offer now: Forget it, and give yourself a year to prepare properly for the marathon.

But there would probably be, I knew, a considerable number of people who would not wait a year, and whose spirit would tell them to get in there and run next March. There would probably be people who would be reasonably fit to begin with anyway, and there would certainly be those who would totally underestimate the sheer distance involved in a marathon. There were, it transpired, all three categories and many more.

But it seemed reasonable that they should at least have the opportunity of following a graduated programme which had tried to make use of the time available as well as possible, even though it would still be like climbing the stairs three at a time.

From the letters I received before and after the London Marathon, it appeared to work, and later in this chapter some of the runners tell their own stories. Their experiences may help to illustrate not just that the 21-week chart itself can work, but, more important, that it is possible to run the marathon distance, given patience and dedication. That also applies, of course, to the 52-week chart which I would prefer you to try. But only you know how important it is for you to run it with less preparation.

You can, incidentally, always elongate the 21-week chart quite simply to suit a period of time lasting anywhere between the 21- and 52-week schedules. All you do is subtract 21 from the total number of weeks you have available – say 26, which would leave you 5. Then count back 5 weeks from Week 20 (skip Week 21 for the moment), which will take you back to Week 16, and mark it.

Start following the schedule normally, but when you reach Week 16, simply repeat each week's programme before moving on, as follows:

Weeks 1.2.3.4.5.6.7.8.9.10.11.12.13.14.15.
16.*16*.17.*17*.18.*18*.19.*19*.20.*20*.21.
Total: 26 weeks.

If your total number of weeks is higher than 40, then repeat the later weeks three times. But always end by doing Week 21 (the taper-down week) just once. And remember that the longer you spend in overall, regular preparation, the greater will be your chances of succeeding.

Some further tips on the crash programme:
* Allow yourself an extra hour's sleep at night. Training for distance running is tiring, and its long-term success depends on a good recovery rate.

* The occasional day off, if you feel you really need it, will do no harm. Otherwise the rest day could be used to replace any session you have had to miss earlier in the week.

* Don't run for three hours after a meal.

* If you have to miss a section, perhaps through illness, gradually pick up where you left off, not where you should have been on the schedule.

* Keep at it. Otherwise the distance will usually win in the end.

Schedule No. 2 The Beginner's Sunday Times *21-Week Crash Programme*

NB Values are in 'running-minutes'

	SUN	MON	TUES	WED	THUR	FRI	SAT
Week 1	10	10	15	10	15	Rest	20
Week 2	25	15	20	15	20	Rest	30
Week 3	35	20	25	20	30	Rest	35
Week 4	40	25	30	20	35	Rest	40
Week 5	45	30	35	20	40	Rest	45
Week 6	50	30	40	25	40	Rest	50
Week 7	55	35	45	25	50	Rest	50
Week 8	60	35	50	25	50	Rest	60
Week 9	70	40	55	30	55	Rest	60
Week 10	80	45	60	30	60	Rest	60
Week 11	90	45	60	35	70	Rest	60
Week 12	100	45	70	35	80	Rest	60
Week 13	105	50	70	40	80	Rest	60
Week 14	110	50	80	40	80	Rest	60
Week 15	120	55	80	40	80	60	Rest

Schedule No. 2 – contd.

	SUN	MON	TUES	WED	THUR	FRI	SAT
Week 16	130	60	80	40	80	60	Rest
Week 17	140	60	80	40	80	60	Rest
Week 18	140	60	90	45	80	60	Rest
Week 19	150	60	80	45	70	60	Rest
Week 20	105	45	70	30	60	Rest	Rest
Week 21	75	15	45	Rest	15	Rest	THE RACE

In the weeks following the publication of that 21-week 'crash' schedule, we were left in no doubt that a good number of readers (and even *Sunday Times* staff) were following the chart carefully. To be honest, the situation filled me with some degree of apprehension, because it meant that in effect I was encouraging in practical terms what I really believed to be inadvisable – the preparation for a marathon by non-runners in little more than five months.

That apprehension did not totally disappear until a short while after the London Marathon, when the accounts of the progress some of the beginner-runners had made in training, which had begun to arrive, were subsequently completed by their experiences of the race itself.

I have picked a cross section of these for inclusion here because each story has its own moral for the beginner, its own inspirational example, and its own warning. Each runner made his own decision to prepare for the London Marathon with little more than a grid of numbers for training guidance. None of them knew any of the others, and at the time I knew none of them either. But their stories exemplify one of the great attractions of the marathon: that in Scotland, or Sussex, or Hertfordshire, or Cornwall, or anywhere, a runner on his or her own can prepare in isolation and can, with dedication, determination and luck, succeed.

Andy Puddicombe, twenty-four, from Gosport, Hants, had left college four months previously and was still unemployed when he decided to use some of the unwanted time on his hands to train for the London Marathon. He had done very little running since leaving school eight years earlier, apart from a couple of miles twice a week training for a local football team.

The marathon had always been a vague ambition, and the thing which excited me most about the chart was that it made it appear actually feasible. I couldn't wait to start! My immediate plan was to begin in Week 5, figuring that I could manage that easily with all the spare time on my hands. But by the end of the week I was shattered, and went straight back to Day 1 of Week 1 next day.

I kept a diary as I went along, and wrote that I was sometimes running too fast in the early weeks on the 20-minute runs and consequently I was more tired after those than after the 40–45 minute runs. In general I was able to complete each week without undue difficulty, and always had a feeling of exultation when I broke new ground, even though it was only five minutes. Week 6 was a bad one, the muscles in my legs were hurting, and at one point I feared that I had a stress fracture. But I was able to run through it, so it couldn't have been that serious, and in fact Weeks 7–10 were about the best of the whole schedule.

In Week 11 I completed the 1½ hours, which proved about the hardest run of all. I was very tired in the last 30 minutes, and quite pessimistic about ever finishing a marathon. It was also the last time I ran an 'out and back' course. I found it quite depressing being so far from home, and I always ran laps of never more than six miles round from then on.

In Weeks 12–15 I was beginning to find the rest day as important as the other six, and I experienced another great feeling of achievement when I ran non-stop for two hours.

Week 16 was something of a watershed in that I had now got a job, and this was my first week of training as well as doing a 40-hour week. It had obviously been a great help being able to choose when to run; also it worked both ways – running helped the drudgery of being unemployed. But it is also probably true that the extra discipline was useful. In the crucial Weeks 16–18 I was so determined not to let work interfere that I probably did slightly more than the schedule.

I got through the 2 hours 10 minutes and 2 hours 20 minutes barriers, but owing partly to a rather hectic social life at the time I became a bit ragged in Weeks 18–20. I had three attempts at the 2½ hours run, never actually giving up on the first two failures, but simply electing halfway round to do a shorter run and postpone the 2½ hour effort. Discipline was definitely waning, as I figured I had already done the hard part. But psychologically I desperately wanted to run 2½ hours before the big day.

With shame I can remember the morning of Sunday, 15 March, exactly a fortnight before the London Marathon, as I stood at the back door, dressed and ready to go out but knowing that it would be quite futile owing to the worst hangover I had suffered for six months. Luckily, that experience quite shook me from my recent lethargy, and I duly completed the 2½ hours run the following day. Thus, Week 20 was a little up and down, but Week 21 was exactly to the schedule.

I always ran alone, but two friends were also training for the race, one copying the schedule, and while we were never rivals it certainly helped having someone with whom to compare notes. I rarely ran in the morning, and was somewhat worried about the 9 a.m. start, but I'm sure it made no difference, as I was up by 6 a.m. on race day.

I never really worried about distances in training, always running to the specified time, but in fact I was nearly always on course for a marathon of 3¼ to 3½ hours. My ill-discipline towards the end prompted me to start with the 3¾ hour starters, but in fact I completed it in 3 hours 20 minutes 8 seconds, placing 2349th. What really pleased me was that my halfway time was 1 hour 37 minutes, so I only slowed up by 6 minutes in the second half. Both my friends, while finishing 5 and 9 minutes faster than me, slowed up by 15–20 minutes in the second half. Both walked at some stage, whereas I ran completely non-stop. Certainly I felt it was important not to go too fast at the start, when it would have been easy to be carried away by the crowd. I was shattered at the end, but within a day I was wondering when and where to run my next one, and was determined to get inside three hours.

Ken Laidler, forty-seven, from Tring, Herts, had taken part in no serious athletics since he left school, although he cycled and played rugby until the age of thirty-eight. Then he stopped, and put on weight. In January 1980 he scaled 10 stones 7 lbs for his height of 5 ft 6½ ins. So he started jogging, and was down to 10 stones 3 lbs by October 1980, when he started following the 21-week schedule with a view to running the London Marathon. By the day of the race itself, five months later, he had trimmed down to 9 stones 3 lbs, and had lost three inches from his waist.

The marathon itself was, he says, a highly emotional experience. 'It took the best part of a week following the race to be able to discuss it rationally and without bringing a lump to my throat. It does seem stupid, a grown man of forty-seven talking this way, but it's true.'

Through his jogging, he was already in advance of Week 1, and had progressed well until just before Christmas.

I was running everything at approximately 8-minute miling pace, and was virtually able to set my watch to it. In most cases, it was a floating sensation. As most of my running had to be in the evenings, and I live in a very small country town, I was unfortunate in that most of my runs took me into dark, badly-lit areas. The pavements were either rough or non-existent, and so I had to run on roadsides which were rough or on the side of steep cambers. This, I am sure, caused a serious knee injury which also affected my two training partners, Bernie and Roy, at the same time. The left knee used to lock.

I went to a physio without much success. I rested it. Little help. Walked and jogged slowly. No effect. And having lost the best part of three weeks training, I decided that I had to just get out and run through it if I was to make the start. If it didn't work then, except for the pain, I would lose nothing.

One of my training partners, Bernie, decided to do the same, but Roy decided against it, and quit. We had to take it easy at first but after about three weeks we ran through it. Every now and again we were given a sharp reminder, but we improved our training conditions by travelling the 7 miles to Aylesbury, and taking advantage of the well-lit streets there. The surfaces were generally better and certainly a lot flatter.

Training was going well again and we were pushing into the unknown each weekend. Now I was beginning to feel stress. Not during the runs themselves, but afterwards. I took longer to recover and felt a little nausea. This only started when I reached distances of 15 miles. I'm sure it was mild dehydration, and we overcame the problem by placing beakers of sugared orange juice and blackcurrant in the hedge along the training circuit so that we were able to take fluid at about 7 and 12 miles, and it worked. No more stress.

However, I found the need every three weeks or so for an extra day's rest. This was obviously fatigue, but I usually found that I then ran my next training session at a faster pace without effort. We got up to 19¾ miles three weeks before the marathon, and were really enjoying our training. It was then time to start tapering down.

I had lost weight (over a stone) and was just a little worried that it was too much, but with six weeks to go it levelled off and even increased slightly during the last two weeks. I was eating well, and luckily my wife Rosalyn (who had thought me mad) entered into the spirit of the thing and cooked me all the right foods. I hadn't had Spotted Dick for years!

The last week before the marathon I had a scare. My daughter had flu. My son had just recovered from it and I had the symptoms of sore throat and headache, but I didn't tell anyone. I just stopped training. All the written advice, including the official medical sheet received with the acceptance, advised against running if you had flu. All that work! I had to be sensible and consider my family, but in the end it had to be my decision. By Saturday I felt better, and decided to give it a go, bearing in mind that I would stop if I should feel any adverse effects.

Well, we started. Gosh, it was fantastic! It took 10 minutes for the first mile as I just had to run with the crowd at Greenwich, but then I got into my 8-minute miles. My rhythm was good, but I had a small blister after only two miles. I was very surprised, but it was no problem and I soon forgot it. I'd started with my training partner Bernie, but we were separated at 8 miles, and did not see each other again. I was running like a bird, just floating, and by 12 miles there were some people around me who were beginning to suffer and didn't want to talk.

Where was that bloody bridge? Someone must have hidden it! I was feeling impatient to get to Tower Bridge, the halfway point, because I knew my wife and close friends would be there, and I was looking forward to seeing them. But we finally reached the Bridge, and they weren't there. I was very disappointed and felt a little low. Then we crossed it and turned right, and there they were: a quick Hello and a wave and I was away again, lifted mightily by their presence.

I reached 15 miles on schedule in 2 hours 6 minutes but realized that fatigue was setting in. By 17 miles, and the Isle of Dogs, I was looking for each mile marker earlier and earlier, and slowing slightly. Then it happened. It seemed as though someone drilled a hole through my hips, put in a long bolt and screwed it up. I hadn't experienced anything like it before. I saw the 18 miles marker. Hell! Another 8 to go. I felt I'd never make it. I tried to run but was reduced to little more than a shuffle. It really hurt, but I had to carry on. There were no underground stations before 20 miles.

Anyway, I had to keep going until we passed The Tower again so that my wife would know I was okay. The pain in the hip was bad though. We passed by Tower Bridge again, crossing those awful cobbles. Now I experienced another phenomenon. I call it Marathon Knee. It wasn't overly painful, but it just didn't seem to function. It was difficult to describe. It was floppy, and tended to give way each step. I had no control. It was like a kind of paralysis.

I was still okay in the upper body, but I had to walk and shuffle for a mile. I saw my wife again and felt happier for a moment. But there were still 3 long miles to go. I closed my eyes. Then I heard a shout: '3-9-2-5! 3-9-2-5!' My number. I thought it must be one of my friends and I opened my eyes. But it was a total stranger, clapping his hands in time as he called out again '3-9-2-5!', and urging me to keep going. Others took up the chant, and for a brief moment so did the crowd. Tears came to my eyes, and I thanked them and kept going. There was no way I could let them down after that. Three more miles of purgatory.

At Big Ben, the blind man passed me. It was his mate I really admired. What a responsibility! I saw Rosalyn again in Birdcage Walk. I was nearly there. And then I finished. Someone gave me a medal. But no-one I knew was there to share my triumph. I fought back the tears.

I couldn't find the bus with my clothes in. I was getting a little annoyed, but it was only fatigue. Eventually I found the right bus, sat down, and felt a little deflated. It was all over. I took off my sodden vest and put on my sweat top. It was impossible to put on my tracksuit trousers. My legs wouldn't move. I just sat there. Where was everyone? My wife? My friends? After five minutes or so they battled through the crowds to reach me. Two men lifted me off the bus. Rosalyn hugged me, and I cried a little. They all hugged me and shook me by the hand. The triumph was complete.

Geoff Hayles, a thirty-six-year-old dental surgeon from Brighton, married with two daughters, developed his marathon interest through the Brighton Hash House Harriers, a social running group which covers 4–8 miles every Monday night.

I played rugby, soccer and swam at school, and after qualifying I played some golf and squash. Three years ago I started jogging occasionally in an attempt to improve my fitness for squash, and a year later joined the Hash House Harriers. But their training runs often clashed with Round Table meetings, and I only went about twenty times in two years. But in spite of the limited outings, I enjoyed running with this jovial group and heard some of the keener ones discussing 10-mile races, half-marathons and marathons. In October 1980 I took part in the Round Table National Sporting Weekend 3½-mile cross country race, and finished 34th out of 83, and shortly afterwards the London Marathon was announced, the schedule appeared in the *Sunday Times*, and I began following it.

Being not averse to a pint or two in good company over the two weeks of the festive season, 1980–81, my body suffered the worst physical assault it has had to endure in its thirty-six years to date. Crying out for sleep, comfort and soothing medicines, the aching head and limbs were forced into action and joggled around the streets and paths of Brighton. And that was near the start of the schedule! This for me was the critical phase, and having survived that I felt confident of keeping the schedule up for a while at least.

It was consoling and encouraging to re-read the advice offered with it at difficult times, and the only part I ignored was when I fell behind schedule (a couple of weekends away from home) and I put in extra time to catch up. That was difficult – 2½ and 3 hours behind at different times, but I felt that if I did every minute of the schedule, my confidence would be that much more. And with my running background, I needed all the confidence I could get!

I found I liked the simplicity of the schedule, and I preferred it being based on time rather than distance. There is a world of difference between knowing you've got to go out and run 10 miles in a certain time, and knowing you can jog along for 20 minutes as slowly as you like. In the latter case, often there is a pleasant surprise at the end, at the distance actually covered.

The low point was always putting the tracksuit on, the high point was soaking in a hot bath afterwards. The ecstasy of heat soaking into aching muscles makes it almost worthwhile on its own.

In February I entered the Woking Athletic Club 10-mile road race to see how I was faring, and finished 475th out of 630 finishers in 65 minutes 38 seconds. In the London Marathon I was around the 3000th mark in 3½ hours, and my wife, Jacky, was so impressed with the London event that she asked for a tracksuit as a present on our next wedding anniversary.

Peter McGough, thirty-one, from Nottingham, had some background of running from 1975, but for the sake of fitness rather than competition. He virtually ceased physical activity between July 1978 and June 1980, as his seventeen-month-old son Michael died of liver disease. During this tragic period, in which the Michael McGough Research Fund for Liver Disease in Children was established, his weight ballooned to 200 lb. He started running again in June 1980, covering 4 miles a day plus circuit-training, and by October 1980 his weight had dropped to 175 lb. The announcement of the London Marathon at that time spurred him to begin the training schedule with a view to raising money for the Research Fund by sponsorship in the marathon.

First of all I copied the routine into a diary to chart my future progress and performance against it. I did not keep pace session for session with the routine, but rather used it as a barometer of the amount of training and peaks I would need to achieve in the pre-marathon period. I felt that as long as I could consistently 'hit' the big Sunday runs, I would be okay.

This is where the routine had its biggest impact on me. I saw that it was not necessary to run ridiculously high mileages in preparation, but what was important was to attain a condition whereby the legs could be kept moving for 2½ hours plus. For a first-timer it also imposed a sense of discipline and commitment to an event which commands respect.

Weeks 1–4: These were okay, as it was not a significant increase on my then current training. I was still maintaining circuit-training, but my plan was to decrease this activity as my running times were upped. As things worked out, I circuit-trained right up to marathon week.

Weeks 5–8: Found it difficult to slow down from my 6 minutes-per-mile pace, and therefore was running too fast, with a high knee lift. Joints began to ache.

Weeks 9–11: The worst period. I over-indulged in food at Christmas and I also caught a virus which I couldn't shake off. I began to have doubts as to whether my entry would be accepted among the 21,000 applications when I realized I had not put a stamp on my final self-addressed acceptance envelope. So it was hard to find motivation for going out on long training runs for an event I might not get into. Net result – no running of any sort. My weight returned to 200 lb.

Weeks 12–13: Recommenced training in Week 12, but at Week 4 targets. I planned to step up in fortnightly increments to get back to actual schedule around Week 18. Motivation still low; sessions missed.

Weeks 14–20: New motivation was received through the letter box: my acceptance form arrived, thanks to an anonymous soul at the GLC who had franked it. Knee and ankle joints began to suffer. I had to shelve plans to go on a crash diet (to reduce weight impact) as my energy levels became very low. I evolved a more economic style of running. I started hitting the schedule targets again in Week 18, and went above thereafter in an effort to catch up some of the previously missed mileage. My major Sunday runs: Week 18: 17 miles in 2 hours 19 minutes; Week 19: 20 miles in 2 hours 53 mins; Week 20: 24 miles in 3 hours 11 minutes. I went beyond the 2½ hour-mark because psychologically I needed to know that I could get nearer the 26 miles.

Week 21: I did not ease down all that gradually, running in total 35 miles ceasing three days before the race. Weight 180 lb.

I found that when running for over an hour or so, I almost went into a 'high', my senses became sharper and more acute, my clarity of thought remarkable. I experienced a tremendous, almost spiritual high during the Marathon too. I went steadily for 18 miles, then finished the last 8 miles 385 yards in under 55 minutes, actually sprinting the last 200 yards. My time was 3 hours 39 minutes 38 seconds, and I finished, full of running, 3658th.

(Peter McGough's run also raised £2000 for the Research Fund.)

David Wilson, thirty-seven, a veterinary surgeon from Dorchester, Dorset, also had marathon dreams. He tells a different story:

Despite the chart, I failed. My training came to an abrupt halt in December on a Monday run which had started off as a normal session, after having had a very good run on the Sunday. I quickly realized that my calf muscles were in trouble, and returned home. I think there was widespread tearing of the muscle fibres but mainly around the medial aspect of the proximal end of the tibia. I had also been in trouble with knee-ache in the hours after running but had tried to ignore this.

(A few days earlier the author had written to him in reply to a training inquiry, and speculated that if he became injured he might have to be put down.)

During all this crash programme, I was never free from aches and pains and would spend the rest of the working day, walking and climbing gates, with great difficulty. Basically my heart and lungs were very good (resting pulse down to 48) but the legs could not keep up – too much, too quickly, too old! – and I refused to listen to warning signs.

After the muscle breakdown I rested, apart from a bit of swimming and a week's walking in the Lake District over the New Year. When my London Marathon entry application form came, it inspired me to have one last try and I had a good relaxed 25-minute run, which was most enjoyable. But then within 24 hours I had knee-ache again which lasted for another week, and resigned myself to having another go next year.

But this is not a tale of woe. It is the start of a new interest, and I am running 25–30 minutes three times weekly (with a constant temptation to go further). I had no running experience before, although I played football until I was twenty-seven. Then for the last ten years, nothing.

My job in a mixed vet practice often means a long day from 8.30 a.m. to 5 p.m. around the farms and stables, and then alternate evenings another 2–3 hours standing during evening surgery. I am sure that this was responsible for my legs having very little recovery time between runs. But the mental effect of a run in the evening away from the telephone was the big bonus. That, and dreaming about the ultimate challenge still to come.

Bill Crotty, a senior sales superintendent for British Telecom, from Uckfield, East Sussex, was just a few months short of his fiftieth birthday when he ran in the 1981 London Marathon. A dabbler at sports after leaving school, he had stopped altogether when he married in 1956, and admitted to having led a very sedentary life for twenty-five years. At the back of his mind, though, was a vague dream about possibly running a marathon one day, inspired by reading accounts of the New York Marathon. He was, to say the least, an unlikely candidate.

When firm plans for the London Marathon were announced, I was still dreaming of taking part, but the training chart and its accompanying article got me started. I felt it was now or never, and I wanted to be in the first real London Marathon. With the chart, which I cut out, I felt I had a starting point and a guide to get me there.

On Monday, 27 October, the day after the chart appeared, I bought my first ever pair of training shoes from Debenhams in Brighton, who had a sale on! They were recommended for road training and racing and turned out to be a super buy because they were so comfortable. I also bought a tracksuit, sweatshirt and waterproof jacket with hood. Thus equipped, I arrived home to impart the good news to my wife that I was about to commence training for the London Marathon. Being a reasonably sane sort of person, she naturally thought I had finally flipped. I changed, and set off on my first training run of Week 1, Day 1: 10 minutes. 5 minutes out and 5 back again. . .

But I couldn't run for 5 minutes! I couldn't believe it. I was exhausted and had to stop for a few minutes' rest. I might add that this was at a very gentle pace, and all my 'running' since then has been at a very gentle pace too. This was a great shock to me, and I decided two things: (1) That I would only take part in the marathon if I was physically fit, and free from any sort of injury; and (2) I would only start if I felt I had a reasonable chance of finishing the course.

I also decided to make it a solo effort. I work in Brighton, which has a first-class athletics club, but I have always felt that athletes tend to look down their noses at people not as good/fit as themselves, and don't really want to know old-timers like me. In any case, I leave home at about 7.30 each morning and return about 5.40 in the evening, and didn't fancy going back into Brighton again last night.

I progressed to some semblance of fitness remarkably quickly following the chart. I had difficulty actually getting out of bed and negotiating the stairs each morning but by the time I got to the office I had usually loosened up again. I trained alone, and because of the dark evenings I had to stay in Uckfield where there is street lighting, pavements or footpaths.

Possibly the worst times were at the start of a run on a frosty, dark evening straight after coming home from work. As I left home with, say, an hour's run in front of me, I wished that I were just finishing. Passing familiar landmarks time after time, night after night, didn't help.

On Christmas Day I went for a 5-mile run, which took about 55 minutes. During this, I turned over my left ankle. It hurt a bit at the time and I almost fell over, but I thought no more of it until the next day when I couldn't run for the pain across the top of my foot. In all, that kept me off the road for ten long days. It was a miserable experience, and I seemed to feel my 'fitness', such as it was, slipping away and with it my chances of taking part in the London Marathon. However, I tried to pick up the chart again, but I couldn't. This depressed me even more.

On Sunday, 18 January, I decided to try a run along part of the new Lewes by-pass. I measured out, by car, a convenient distance of 5.2 miles

(2.6 there, and 2.6 back again). I then ran, and couldn't believe my eyes when I saw my time of just under 45 minutes. Allowing for a bit of error all round, this was 5 × 9 minute miles – fabulous running for me, I can tell you, and a real boost.

I felt great, and decided that Cliff Temple and his chart were too tough for me! It seemed to me to be too much to expect myself to do. I thought the chart was all right for people who had done some running, no matter how minimal, before. I had given it a good try but I couldn't cope with it, and that was all there was to that. Instead, I decided to carry on running regularly and try to build up a good mileage. I stuck to the idea of running six days a week and I also tried to do reasonably high weekly mileages because I believed the warning about the Distance beating me otherwise.

Then, would you believe it, on Wednesday, 28 January, I turned over my right ankle (the left foot was still a bit dodgy so I may have been favouring it and brought this second injury on myself). I knew that I, of all people, could not afford another ten days off the road. I even began to hope my entry would not be accepted. I went to a physiotherapist, who told me it was nothing really, just a minor injury to my 'triangular' ligament. He couldn't feel the pain I felt, of course. He was marvellous, and I was back running again (minus a few quid) on Monday, 2 February.

On Sunday, 8 February, I did my Lewes by-pass 5 miles again, in wind and rain. It was tough but I enjoyed it and despite awful conditions ran it in 45 minutes again. It was another confidence booster, but I couldn't help thinking that 5 miles is a lot different from 26-plus, and I wasn't going to make it. A week later I completed 10 miles on the good old Lewes by-pass (what would I have done without it?) in 1 hour 40 minutes. 10 × 10 minute miles – a major achievement for me. I was on top of the world.

By now the evenings were a little lighter, so I was able to run along badly surfaced footpaths on the A22 to the next village and back for about 7 miles total. I also mapped out a 10-mile circuit, with two 5-mile laps shaped like a figure eight, at Crawley.

I completed my longest training run, 15 miles, at Crawley on 12 March in just under 2 hours 40 minutes, or about 10½-minute miles. I felt reasonable at the end of it but very apprehensive about carrying on for another 11 miles; in fact, I had grave doubts that I could do it. But I felt I'd come this far so I might as well continue.

I took a week's leave beginning Monday, 16 March, to wind up my training with a hard week of between 50–60 miles. I then planned to have a quiet week leading up to the big day. It didn't work out like that, perhaps because I switched to morning runs. On Monday I just could not get into the right frame of mind. It took all my self-control to force me to keep going for a 50-minute 5-mile run. Tuesday and Wednesday were only marginally better with a 75-minute 7½-mile spin each day. However, the Wednesday run left me with a sore Achilles tendon – something I had never experienced before and at this late stage somewhat frightening. I didn't run at all on Thursday as a precautionary measure and only did a very easy 4 miles on Friday. Another day off on Saturday and I ended the week on a better note with a 140-minute run of 13½ miles on Sunday.

I felt no more ill-effects from the tendon, but after that easy Friday run I finished with the skin under and between the toes of my left foot cracked and painful to walk on. (I covered them in Vaseline before the Sunday run which did the trick.) I had hoped for so much during that week and finished with a miserable 37½ miles plus a bit of foot trouble. My morale was at an all-time low now. I really felt bad because it seemed to me that things had gone wrong so late that I didn't have time to put them right again.

As you will have gathered I am no runner. All I wanted was to finish in 5 hours (as I had put on my entry form). I had planned to start off the marathon at about 11-minute mile pace and reckoned this would give me enough time in hand in the second half to reach my target time. Since I reached a reasonable level of fitness my speed had not increased. Although it can be argued that from not being able to run for five minutes to being able to run 15 miles in under 2¾ hours is an infinite improvement, I turned out 10-minute miles all the time. In fact, they became so regular that I got to the stage where I felt I could confidently go out anywhere and run for an hour and it would be a distance of 6 miles! However, I could not improve on that. There are two ways to tackle a marathon, one is to run around and the other is to jog around, which is what I wanted, but this last week undermined my confidence to such an extent that I didn't believe I was capable of doing even that.

I stuck to my plans for an easy last week, going for my final winding-up run on Tuesday, 24 March. I went out straight from work on a miserable grey misty day. It had been like this all day so I just went out in my tracksuit, up the A27 from Brighton to Lewes (via pavement and footpath). After a while it began to drizzle and by the time I reached Lewes it was raining properly. As I turned to run back to Brighton it began to pour, and I was running into the wind. I finished soaked to the skin and cold but I felt great (funny game this running!) and the 12½ miles had been covered in 2 hours 5 minutes. Incredible. Everything was together again, the Vaseline had worked and once again in awful conditions I never once felt like giving up.

The next day I awoke with a painful back, I thought. Actually it was the left shoulder. At lunchtime I bought a pair of shorts, running socks and vest for the big day. I had never owned these before and left the purchase of them so late because I didn't want to buy them and then not run. On Thursday 26 March I had a short run to try out the shorts and vest. Every time my left foot hit the ground the shoulder hurt, and I felt very conspicuous in shorts and vest! I was in fact full of trepidation about running the marathon in shorts and vest. I believed I would get cold, as I had always run in my tracksuit. Anyhow that was my training, for better or for worse, wrapped up.

My wife and I stayed at one of the Trust House Forte hotels on the Saturday night and shared a taxi to Greenwich with another runner on Sunday morning. We didn't attend the famous pasta party, and I just ate normally all the way through my training. We both thought the organization for the start and all the way through was magnificent.

At the start I felt the usual butterflies in my tummy but the shoulder was OK as was everything else – plenty of Vaseline on my feet and a thin green woolly over my vest to keep me warm. A couple of thirty-two-year-old men from another part of my office had also entered. On the Friday before the race I told one of them I was in it and he found me as we lined up to start. I didn't really want to run with him as he is seventeen years younger than me, big, strong and fit (football and cricket non-stop for about seventeen years now). The first 6 miles he stayed back with me and consequently I went far too fast for my plan (one hour). It happened again with the next 7 miles too, covered in about 70 minutes. 15 miles came up in 2½ hours. 15 × 10 minute miles! Much too quick for me and I was beginning to worry a little at the fast pace (for me). I ran for a while with a girl who said she hoped to finish in about 3½ hours. She was worried about the bleakness of the Isle of Dogs portion, and said the furthest she had run in training was 14 miles. I lost sight of her when on two occasions I slowed for drinks but she kept on going. I looked for her name among the finishers but I couldn't find it. I hope she made it.

I took a drink at almost every feeding station. I missed the 17-mile sign and by 18 was suffering and couldn't read my watch (I ran without my specs and what with the rain and perspiration I had difficulty reading the dial). Just after 18 miles I couldn't run any more, so I walked for a while. Once again I had no thoughts of giving up. I felt that after five months of training and having made it to 18 miles I was home and dry even if it took me the rest of the day. I enjoyed the champagne provided by the Wapping Wine Store and thought the marina at the St Catherine's Dock looked great.

I walked for a while, then ran for a while. Breaking into a jog again after walking was murder but once I made the effort I managed to keep going for a fair bit. I hated the cobbles at the Tower, but from there onwards it was roses all the way. At about the 24 miles mark I began to feel intoxicated as I knew there was nothing on earth that could stop me from finishing. All the way around the spectators had been wonderful. From the beginning they had encouraged us. I couldn't have retired in front of them even if I'd wanted to. They clapped and cheered all the way. I did the same to them. I told hundreds that they were 'winners' too to stand out in the rain for hours to watch a bunch of rag, tag and bobtails like us, and they were.

When I turned into Birdcage Walk the crowd lifted me with a great roar. I was able to respond and ran up past the Palace feeling 10 feet tall. I was cheered all the way and my wife (who had begun to think I was on a bus somewhere) says she couldn't believe the way I finished. She said it quite brought a lump to her throat and a tear to her eye.

I suppose the icing on the cake was to hear the announcer at the finish booming out: 'And here comes Bill Crotty from Uckfield, in East Sussex, finishing his first-ever marathon, in under 5 hours.'

I could hardly believe this was happening to me. My official time was 4 hours 46 minutes 53 seconds. Steve Ovett never felt better than me! I finished 6243rd of those timed by computer (out of 6255). Another 163 finished behind me, and 637 retired. It was the best day of my life. I was on Cloud Nine. At last I'd done something almost unique, and I still keep the medal with me everywhere I go, like a big kid.

Of course it will wear off, or some of it, but I feel I have something in common with world class athletes, and Olympic gold medallists. I've run a marathon! I didn't beat many people; I didn't expect to, and I didn't set out to. But I did beat 26 miles 385 yards. Nobody can take that away from me.

4

Further Along the Road

The 24-Week Build-Up Programme for the Active Club Athlete

Another type of runner, distinct from those who have little or no running background, is the club athlete who has already been active for some time, competes regularly in shorter road races, and has long been toying with the idea of running a marathon without actually taking the plunge. He or she has the advantage of a reasonable running background, knowledge of the sport and personal abilities and limitations, and an experience of racing. But so far he or she might not have managed to sustain training at a level high enough to feel ready to tackle a marathon (even though such a runner is probably much fitter than many of those who have already run the distance).

For many years I was in this category myself. As a schoolboy runner devoid of speed, I could hardly wait to be old enough to run a marathon and firmly intended to find one as soon as possible after my twenty-first birthday (as the age limit then was). When I reached twenty-one, I decided to get somewhat fitter first, and stuck to 10-milers. Year after year, as my fitness rose and fell, it never quite reached the point where I was satisfied with it. I ran the Finchley 20-mile road race in 1974 in 2 hours 3 minutes, but the last 5 miles were hard. I needed to get fitter for the extra 6, I decided. Instead, I became less fit. It was another four years – ten years later than I'd planned – before I finally lined up for that first marathon at the age of thirty-one. And then I wished I'd done so long before.

So the next training schedule is designed for the 'almost' marathon runner. The athlete who hovers around 30–40 miles a week of mainly steady running, turns out for the club most weekends, and finishes down in the pack somewhere. Not a prize-winner. Not a star. Perhaps even rather directionless in approach.

But with a bit of a push, a potential sub-3-hour marathon runner. Don't waste time like I did. This is for you.

If you have read the beginners' charts on pages 45–50, the first difference you will notice with this one is that the sessions are given mainly in miles rather than 'running-minutes'. Most club runners have a reasonable idea of distance, and probably have their own regular training routes of different lengths anyway.

But the overall pattern is the same. The long run on Sunday, gradually increasing in length over the training period to acclimatize the body to simply running for that length of time. Then the rest of the week is divided between medium sessions, with the second-longest run of the week normally coming on the Wednesday. Club races also play their part, with a gradual increase in competition distance as fitness builds up.

To provide more training variety, and to allow for a faster training pace on some days, two shorter sessions are suggested, or else a period of *fartlek* (the Swedish word for speedplay) in which the runner surges, sprints and jogs as he feels, rather than on a pre-set pattern. Again, this provides a mental relief as well as a change of pace, although it must never be forgotten that the marathon itself requires a steady, economic effort and the sudden bursts of speed are in the main best kept for training.

A weekly run including hills is also part of the schedule. This can either be carried out on a particularly hilly course, where the gradients are a natural part of the run, or else as a deliberate session of running up a steep hill, then jogging back down, and repeating six to eight times during the middle of a run. The point to always remember with any interval hill work, though, is to run right over the top of the hill for a short distance before you stop and turn. It is a good habit to develop, for otherwise your body starts looking for an automatic rest after a climb during a race.

Again, the schedule allows for one rest day a week, although when the mileage gets to its heaviest this is not always possible.

So make particular efforts at that time to get proper sleep and relaxation, to keep late night socializing to a reasonable minimum, to offset the possible cumulative effects of fatigue and to try to reduce the likelihood of injury.

Incidentally, I make no concession to the female runner in this schedule. Her pace may be slower, but the marathon she runs is exactly the same distance as the men's, so the quantity of training is exactly the same.

Schedule No. 3
The 24-Week Build-Up Programme for the Active Club Athlete

	APPROX. WEEKLY MILEAGE TOTAL	SUN	MON	TUES	WED	THUR	FRI	SAT
Week 1	40	10 miles	6 miles fartlek	4 miles	8 miles	5 miles	Rest	7 miles
Week 2	45	11 miles	7 miles fartlek	5 miles	8 miles	7 miles	Rest	7 miles
Week 3	50	12 miles	8 miles	5 miles fast	9 miles	6 miles	Rest	RACE: 10 miles
Week 4	55	12 miles	8 miles	6 miles fast	9 miles	8 miles	Rest	2 × 6 miles
Week 5	60	12 miles	8 miles	8 miles fast	9 miles	8 miles	5 miles	RACE: 10 miles
Week 6	60	14 miles	8 miles	6 miles fast	10 miles	2 × 6 miles	Rest	10 miles
Week 7	65	14 miles	2 × 5 miles	8 miles fast	10 miles	2 × 6 miles	Rest	11 miles
Week 8	55	15 miles	8 miles	6 miles fast	10 miles	6 miles	Rest	RACE: 10 miles
Week 9	65	15 miles	2 × 5 miles	8 miles fast	12 miles	8 miles	Rest	12 miles
Week 10	70	16 miles	2 × 5 miles	10 miles incl. hills	12 miles	10 miles fartlek	Rest	12 miles
Week 11	65	16 miles	2 × 5 miles	10 miles incl. hills	12 miles	1 hour fartlek	Rest	RACE: 10 miles
Week 12	75	17 miles	2 × 5 miles	10 miles incl. hills	12 miles	2 × 6 miles	Rest	8 miles + 6 miles

	APPROX. MILEAGE TOTAL	SUN	MON	TUES	WED	THUR	FRI	SAT
Week 13	65	17 miles	8 miles	10 miles incl. hills	12 miles	1 hour fartlek	Rest	RACE: 10–12 miles
Week 14	80	18 miles	8 miles	10 miles incl. hills	14 miles	1 hour fartlek	2 × 5 miles	12 miles
Week 15	70	18 miles	2 × 5 miles	10 miles incl. hills	12 miles	1 hour fartlek	Rest	RACE: 10–13 miles
Week 16	85	20 miles	2 × 5 miles	10 miles incl. hills	14 miles	1 hour fartlek	9 miles	8 miles + 6 miles
Week 17	80	20 miles	2 × 6 miles	10 miles incl. hills	14 miles	1 hour fartlek	6 miles	10 miles
Week 18	75	18 miles	2 × 5 miles	10 miles incl. hills	12 miles	1 hour fartlek	4 miles	RACE: 12–15 miles
Week 19	90	12 miles	2 × 6 miles	10 miles incl. hills	15 miles	1 hour fartlek	7 miles + 4 miles	22 miles
Week 20	60	10 miles + 8 miles	5 miles	8 miles incl. hills	12 miles	1 hour fartlek	4 miles + 5 miles	Rest
Week 21	70	RACE: 20 miles	8 miles	10 miles incl. hills	14 miles	1 hour fartlek	2 × 5 miles	Rest
Week 22	80	22–24 miles	5 miles	10 miles incl. hills	14 miles	1 hour fartlek	2 × 5 miles	10 miles
Week 23	50–60	15 miles	5 miles	8 miles incl. hills	10 miles	6 miles	Rest	6 miles
Week 24	50	10 miles	Rest	6 miles incl. hills	6 miles	Rest	2 miles jog	THE RACE

The Ambitious International Runner

So we come to the élite marathon runner, the serious competitor, whose aim is not simply to complete the distance, but to do so faster than anyone else, even if it means doing so at well under 5-minute-mile pace for every single mile.

Whereas a good club-level runner may run 15–20 miles on a Sunday, the serious runner is someone who covers that distance every single day of the week. Not always in one session, but as part of a regular routine which will mean training twice or even three times a day. And while a club runner may fit his training around his work, often the very ambitious runner will prefer, or need, to fit his work around his training.

What exactly constitutes the right training for an ambitious runner? Every athlete has his or her own answer, and there is the intriguing possibility that the perfect method simply may not yet have been discovered. But, far more likely, the perfect method to suit everyone simply could not exist. What each runner has to discover, therefore, is a personal ideal method through trial, error and more trial.

So the search for that correct balance of hard, easy, fast, slow training continues the world over. Ron Hill, the former European and Commonwealth champion, and one of the marathon's most successful experimentalists and innovators, suggests that we may be coming close to the optimum performance in the event. 'People talk about the possibility of a 2-hour marathon, but I think 2 hours 5 minutes would be a more realistic limit,' he says. 'And we're not even nibbling at that yet. When it is reached, it will be done by a 10,000 metres runner who is motivated towards the marathon. When I ran my fastest time of 2 hours 9 minutes 28 seconds, I went through 10 miles in 47:45, and the next 10 miles in under 50 minutes.

'But unless doctors find a method, or evolution results in bigger people with longer legs, we'll never get down to 2 hours. I think it's impossible simply because I don't believe the human body is capable of carrying that much energy store in available glycogen or fat.'

Approaches to training do change. A 1920 newspaper reported that four US runners had completed their preparation for the Olympic marathon in Antwerp by running round the whole course in 2 hours 46 minutes 55 seconds just eleven days before the race itself.

Yet at the Games, the best-placed of them, Joe Organ, was 7th in only 2:41.30, with Carl Linder 11th in 2:44.21 and Charles Mellor 12th in 2:45.30, and it seems likely that they had already left too much of their form on the road. These days no one would dream of running the whole course eleven days before a marathon in a time so close to their best, and still expect to be fresh for the race itself. (Incidentally, my favourite 1920 Olympian must be the other American, Arthur Roth, who started that training run with them, broke a shoelace after 20 miles, and while hurrying to catch up was knocked out when a careless Belgian peasant opened a door in his face. Now I can identify with that. And he didn't finish the Olympic race either.)

The training chart on page 70 shows a typical 16-week schedule for an athlete who is already training at a high level, and has an important marathon coming up. There are dozens of possible variations on such a chart, but I prefer to keep basically to the principle of hard/easy weeks in the belief that recovery afforded by a relatively low-mileage week is even more essential at this level than during a much more modest programme.

Too often, it seems, the ambitious athlete fears that to drop, even briefly, below a certain quantity of training will mean impending disaster. But I feel the opposite is true: *not* to drop below a certain level, and give the body a chance to recover and repair before the next hard week, is tempting fate in terms of injury. The motto: hard work plus rest equals success.

For not only is such a volume of running extremely hard, but relaxation in between is equally important. Too much stress at work, too much travelling, or overtime, or irregular hours, or the actual physical demands of the job, may not necessarily ruin the really determined runner's training progress. But they certainly won't help either.

Yes, I know that it is easy for me to say, 'Give up your job because it involves a stressful 80-minute rush-hour rail journey every day,' or 'Don't do two hours' overtime because a 10-mile run will have greater benefit for your marathon training,' while conveniently overlooking that you may have a mortgage and bills to pay, mouths to feed, and a career to sustain. Rationally, it may be quite ludicrous to even think of putting your livelihood and your family's comfort in jeopardy, simply so that you can go out and run 10 miles in the hope that eventually you may be able to run it faster than the next man.

Schedule No. 4
The Ambitious International Runner (16-Week Build-Up)

	APPROX. MILEAGE TOTAL		SUN	MON	TUES	WED	THUR	FRI	SAT
Week 1		am	18 miles	5 miles	7 miles	7 miles	7 miles	7 miles	5 miles
	80	pm	—	8 miles fast	6 × 1 mile 5 mins jog between	8 miles	8 × 600 m on track, 200 m jog	—	Low key 5 miles race
Week 2	90	am	20 miles	5 miles	5 miles	5 miles	5 miles	8 miles	5 miles
		pm	—	8 miles fast	7 miles	12 miles	6 × 1000 m on track, 200 m jog	—	Low key race?
Week 3	100	am	20 miles	6 miles	5 miles	7 miles	5 miles	10 miles	5 miles
		pm	—	8 miles fast	9 miles	12 miles	6 × 800 m on track, 200 m jog	—	8 miles
Week 4	95	am	20 miles	5 miles	7 miles	—	7 miles	7 miles	10 miles
		pm	—	8 miles fast	6 × 1 mile 5 min jog	12 miles	8 × 600 m on track, 200 m jog	—	Low key race?
Week 5	110	am	20 miles	5 miles	7 miles	5 miles	7 miles	5 miles	12 miles
		pm	5 miles	9 miles fast	6 × 1 mile, 5 mins jog	12 miles	6 × 1000 m on track, 200 m jog	—	6 miles

Schedule No.4 contd.

	APPROX. MILEAGE TOTAL		SUN	MON	TUES	WED	THUR	FRI	SAT
Week 6	90	am	20 miles	5 miles	5 miles	5 miles	5 miles	5 miles	—
		pm	—	7 miles fast	6 × 1 mile, 5 mins jog	12 miles	8 × 800 m on track, 200 m jog	—	10 miles ROAD RACE
Week 7	120	am	22 miles	7 miles	5 miles	7 miles	7 miles	10 miles	5 miles
		pm	4 miles	10 miles fast	6 × 1 mile, 5 mins jog	12 miles	8 × 600 m on track, 200 m jog	—	HALF MARATHON RACE
Week 8	100	am	20 miles	5 miles	7 miles	5 miles	7 miles	5 miles	10 miles
		pm	5 miles	7 miles fast	6 × 1 mile 5 mins jog	12 miles	8 × 800 m on track, 200 m jog	—	—
Week 9	120	am	22 miles	7 miles	5 miles	7 miles	5 miles	7 miles	10 miles
		pm	5 miles	10 miles fast	6 × 1 mile, 5 mins jog	15 miles	6 × 1000 m on track, 200 m jog	5 miles	5 miles
Week 10	100	am	24 miles	5 miles	5 miles	7 miles	5 miles	7 miles	—
		pm	—	6 miles fast	6 × 1 mile, 5 mins jog	15 miles	8 × 800 m on track, 200 m jog	—	10 miles RACE

Schedule No.4 contd.

	APPROX. MILEAGE TOTAL		SUN	MON	TUES	WED	THUR	FRI	SAT
Week 11	130	am	24 miles	7 miles	7 miles	7 miles	7 miles	7 miles	12 miles
		pm	5 miles	10 miles fast	8 × 1 mile, 5 mins jog	15 miles	8 × 600 m on track, 200 m jog	—	6 miles
Week 12	100	am	22 miles	5 miles	5 miles	5 miles	5 miles	3 miles	—
		pm	—	5 miles fast	6 × 1 mile, 5 mins jog	12 miles	6 × 1000 m on track, 200 m jog	—	20 miles ROAD RACE
Week 13	140	am	15 miles	8 miles / 5 miles	8 miles	5 miles	8 miles / 5 miles	7 miles / 5 miles	10 miles
		pm	5 miles	10 miles	10 miles	15 miles	10 miles	8 miles	6 miles
Week 14	100	am	22 miles	—	5 miles	5 miles	7 miles	5 miles	—
		pm	—	7 miles fast	6 × 1 mile, 5 mins jog	15 miles	8 × 800 m on track, 200 m jog	—	10 miles ROAD RACE
Week 15	70	am	20 miles	5 miles	5 miles	—	5 miles	5 miles	—
		pm	—	7 miles fast	—	12 miles	6 × 1000 m on track, 200 m jog	—	5 miles ROAD RACE
Week 16	75	am	15 miles	—	5 miles	—	2 miles jog	2 miles jog	THE
		pm	—	7 miles fast	6 × 600 m 5 mins jog	10 miles	—	—	RACE

The theory of amateur sport is admirable: You have a job and a domestic situation, and in your spare time you can engage in some physical recreation like running to keep fit, and for a little friendly competition and socializing in off-duty hours. For a lot of people that is exactly how it is, and how it should be, and the saddest part is that many others do not even take *that* amount of physical exercise.

But the theory is not always so practical when we are talking about people who want very much (for whatever reason) to become one of the finest exponents of long distance running in the entire world. Bearing in mind the intense competition, it is plain that to reach such a level is going to take more than a casual half-hour here and there.

As you get nearer and nearer to that goal, so running encroaches on every working, domestic and social activity to some degree, and whether or not you succeed may depend a very great deal on how understanding and supportive are your immediate family and friends. If your disappearance out of the front door on a training run is habitually followed very shortly afterwards by a torrent of abuse, a vase of flowers, the clock, and Fluffy the Cat, and you are met on your return by your burnt dinner at head height, then the chances are that you are probably not receiving sufficient sympathetic backing from home in your endeavour.

A survey of competitors in the 1980 New York City Marathon showed, in common with other obsessive people, a divorce rate 3½ times higher than for non-runners with similar backgrounds. 'The key difference between a person who becomes an addict and one who uses running sensibly, is moderation,' says Dr Michael Sacks, Associate Professor at Cornell Medical School. 'But many marathon runners train by doing 70–100 miles a week. A married addict will start to pay less attention to his spouse. Some totally change their lifestyle to accommodate what is supposed to be a leisure-time activity. They change their diet, their clothes, their friends, their attitude to their careers and, in some cases, even their spouse.' That was an American survey, and by no means automatically applicable in the UK. But don't say you haven't been warned!

Running can also, of course, be a shared activity. Ian Thompson's wife, Margaret, is a former holder of the UK women's marathon best, and they take it in turns to baby-sit while the other goes out training. Joyce Smith's husband, Bryan, is also her coach, and when their two daughters were younger, he also looked after them whenever Joyce trained. It just takes a little organization.

As far as a career goes, there is no doubt that many leading athletes (and not only marathon runners) have in the past turned down possible promotion or even a better job because it would leave them less time for training. Or they simply never had the chance for promotion in the first place because they rarely worked overtime, or were so frequently away from work on overseas athletics trips, often without pay.

Every individual has to weigh up the various considerations and decide whether he is willing to put in an attempt to reach international class as an athlete ahead of his career. It is not an easy question, bearing in mind that there are no guarantees that concentration on marathon running will produce the results required. And even if it does, there still may be little or no opportunity to benefit financially from the success.

Hopefully, the amateur rules may soon unbend more than they have already, and it may eventually be possible for a top marathon runner to pick up as much from prizemoney, appearance money and advertising as the world's top golfers and tennis players do now. But even potential pro golfers and tennis players have to make a decision at some point as to whether, and when, they should turn full-time professional, and any change in the amateur rules of athletics is certainly not going to turn every sub-2:20 marathon runner into a millionaire within a month.

Above all, the consideration of how much you want running to dictate your life should really include as a high priority the very relevant question: 'Am I, or could I be, good enough?'

You really need to recognize a burning feeling inside you that it *is* only the restriction of work, or whatever, which is holding you back. There must be some signs of your ability to become a good runner, for it might be totally irresponsible to risk jeopardizing a career in an endeavour to become a great athlete when the basic ability is plainly not there in the first place. But then again that ability is less essential in the marathon than in, say, the sprints, where you need to have been born with a considerable amount of natural speed.

Some athletes in the USA have already made a virtual profession out of being runners, as some of the biggest road races there pay considerable undercover appearance money to the top athletes, plus, occasionally, hard prizemoney. All quite illegal, according to the rule book, but accepted practice where major sponsors are footing the bill.

And there are fringe activities, like selling brand name running shoes and tracksuits. Both Bill Rodgers, four-times winner of the Boston Marathon and a three-times winner at New York, and the 1972 Olympic marathon champion Frank Shorter have their names on their own particular line of highly successful running gear.

Rodgers, in an April 1981 interview with the *New York Times*, estimated that, 'Last year, from my clothing line, my three running stores, writing for *The Runner* magazine, clinics, after-dinner speaking, sales meetings, and things like that, I made $200,000 to $250,000 before taxes. I think I'm paying $150,000 in taxes this year, including carry-over from previous years. It's a change from 1976, when I made only $10,000 as a teacher. I'm obviously in a very fortunate position, and I'm aware of it.'

In Britain, however, the opportunities to make any form of living from road running are as yet virtually non-existent, and track and field stars probably do considerably better in that respect. But it may change, and then an event like the London Marathon would become worth a great deal of money to the winner: not *directly*, but through the vast media exposure given to the event. In the US, top athletes would be falling over themselves to compete in such a nationally covered race because of the 'high visibility factor' it would afford them. If they did well, their market value to other events, which paid appearance money, would increase, and so would marketing opportunities.

The famous Boston Marathon, which still sticks rigidly to its traditions of extending no formal invitations, paying no expense money (let alone appearance money) and no undercover prizemoney, remains a popular race with leading US athletes, despite their having to pay their own way there, because of the national 'exposure' it offers.

But in turn some of the US runners are probably now tempted into over-racing, motivated by cash and the widest media-exposure available rather than following a sensible training and racing programme.

This is an area where the introduction of open athletics could affect Britain, or indeed any country, as the financial rewards soared. For instance, even if the amateur rules do not change further, the financial value to any American runner winning the marathon in the 1984 Olympics at Los Angeles would probably be inestimable.

And through his own running-related income, Bill Rodgers has also developed an almost perfect training routine, which allows him to sleep late, and train at 10.30 a.m. or 11 a.m., and again at 5 p.m.

'In a typical week, I train twice a day, covering about 10–13 miles in the morning, and 8–10 miles at night. On average it works out to about 130 miles a week, or 18 miles a day. Once a week I do a track session of interval quarter, half or three-quarter miles, with a 220-yard jog, or perhaps six repetition miles at about 4 minutes 45 seconds each. Then I do a long run of about 18–20 miles each week at about 6 minutes 30 seconds pace with another run at night of 5–10 miles perhaps a little quicker. What you really need is a well-rounded programme, with the rest, the distance and the speedwork all put together in the right combination.'

It was not always like that for the top road runners, even in the USA, where marathoners were thought, as in Britain, to be cranky introverts on the outside of the sport. Now they are more widely recognized as cranky introverts on the inside of the sport.

But above all, the commercialization of marathoning there has not exactly made the top runners cover the distance any faster. Simply more often. It still comes back to that need for an inner determination which money itself cannot buy. Among the best marathon men of the past, who usually earned not a penny, that always existed anyway, and was reflected in their training.

Although Bill Adcocks from Coventry has not run a marathon for ten years, for instance, his training and competitive approach are still of great relevance and interest today because few other British runners have even neared his best times of 2 hours 10 minutes 48 seconds (winning the 1968 Fukuoka classic in Japan) and 2 hours 11 minutes 8 seconds (set in winning the 1969 Athens Marathon, which was described by one world authority in 1981 as probably the best marathon performance ever, in view of the difficult course and conditions).

He was Commonwealth Games silver medallist in 1966, and finished fifth in the 1968 Mexico City Olympic marathon, despite the 7000-feet altitude. Injury ended his marathon career in 1972, but fortunately he is still active in the sport as Midland Counties

Marathon Coach, and Chairman of the British Marathon Runners Club. He says:

Most people who come into contact with me for whatever reason appreciate that I'm a fairly intense bloke, and most probably some of my ideas were quite intense. One of the disadvantages of that is that you stand a greater chance of being injured and foreshortening your career, and in retrospect I most probably did. I paid the price through injury, but I got something out of it in terms of doing as well as I think I was able to do, and I think that at the end of the day, no matter what level you run, that is the most important consideration, and it is the decision you have to make.

With more and more marathons taking place, particularly abroad, perhaps some athletes aren't as discriminating now in their choice of races as they used to be. They tend to run more races than they should to get the most out of themselves.

In my career, I never ran a 'small' marathon. Every race in which I ran had some significance, such as a title at stake, or selection for an international race. Even then I was often aware that someone had paid x number of pounds for my air fare to a race and I always felt a responsibility to do as well as I could. Now it seems there is a little more of the 'well, there's another race next week' attitude. All together, I started in eighteen marathons between 1964 and 1972, and finished fifteen of them.

The most training I ever did in a week was 141 miles just before we went to the Mexico Olympics, but on average when I was training hard, I'd cover 120–125 miles a week. It's difficult to equate that with what other people do, because you should always be working out what you should be doing yourself rather than worrying about others. I think this is where some of the injury breakdown comes about: people trying to do too much for their own bodies, because they hear someone else is doing so many miles a week.

I'd run for eleven years before my first marathon, which I ran at Port Talbot in 2 hours 19 minutes 28 seconds, on an average of 80 miles training a week. People always ask me what sort of training I was doing when I was running at my best, but it's what you do in the five to six years before that which is really important. How have you got where you are? It's not just one winter of work, but almost a lifetime which brings you to a peak. It's not like switching on an electric light bulb.

My furthest-ever training run was 25 miles, just once, but normally I'd run 22 miles on a Sunday morning. A group of us would cover it in 2 hours 10 minutes in the weeks after the National Cross Country championship in March, then gradually bring the time down to 1 hour 58 minutes. Except one week when Derek Clayton came up and knocked that into a cocked hat, and we ran it in about 1 hour 52 minutes!

I had a number of regular training courses, like an 11-mile route I used to do on a Monday night at anything between 54 and 58 minutes. Often on a Tuesday I'd do the equivalent of 3 × 7 miles with 4 hours' rest in between. I'd run before work, at lunchtime and after work, which is really the same principle of interval training as a 1500 metres-runner covering 12 × 400 metres in 58 seconds with 2 minutes' rest in between.

The week before a race, I'd run 15 miles on the Sunday instead of 22. Most people latch on to something they've done prior to their best time in the past. When I ran that 2:10 in Fukuoka I'd gone out with some others on the Wednesday before the race and, on a really terrible day, wet and windy, we covered it in about 53 minutes, which was quite fast for a 10 before a race, and then eased off.

From that race onwards, I always liked to go out and have a good, hard run on the Wednesday. It's interesting that I can talk about my former training habits to physiologists today, and they can tell me the whys and wherefores of how I felt. I can identify with the things to which they now put scientific names. But it seems ironic that it's taken the scientists so long to catch up.

There's a saying that 'you don't have to be mad, but it helps', and there is an element of madness in such hard training. If you're not looking for something different, if you're content to just do what other people do, then you may be lucky and it may pay off anyway. But I don't believe I was a particularly good runner. I was just mad enough, and had the drive and determination to keep going. When things went wrong, that was usually the spur to get back, where some others might drop off in the face of adversity. It's very finely balanced. In a race two blokes might physically be of very similar fitness, but there will be something in their personalities which will make the difference. One will have a greater inner determination.

You have to plan a year-round programme, and put in some lighter training periods yourself. If you don't, they'll be put in for you by breakdown through injury. It's like a sentence and punctuation. You either decide yourself where to put in the commas and full stops to best effect, or someone else does it haphazardly and changes the whole meaning. And you have to know yourself. I can remember seeing some blokes going out on the track for a speed session on the Tuesday after a marathon. They were capable of it, but was that the best thing for them at that stage of recovery?

I always accepted that if I were going to run a marathon, then it was damn well going to hurt, and I knew that if anything went wrong, then it would be sheer purgatory. One way to avoid that would have been to run slow, of course. But if you're in the game to run fast, that's not much use.

Now we're trying to put too much emphasis on looking for an easy way – carbohydrate loading, special drinks, shoes, or whatever – to make us run faster. They may help. But it still comes down to having to run hard, whatever you've eaten, or have on your feet.

Ron Hill has been the most durable British marathon runner in recent years, as well as one of the most successful. After some disappointing experiences at the distance early in his international career, he refined, and learned from his mistakes to win the 1969 European and 1970 Commonwealth Games marathon titles, ran a European best of 2 hours 9 minutes 28 seconds, became the only Briton to win the Boston Marathon, ran under 2 hours 13 minutes five times, and developed such innovations as the mesh vest and the carbohydrate loading diet for marathon runners.

He is also still a fanatical trainer, in terms of regularity as much as quantity, and he has not missed training twice a day (once on Sundays) since 20 December 1964. Every one of some 100,000 training miles is neatly recorded in log books going back to 1956. 'A couple of miles is usually what I qualify as a minimum run. But I would say that training is when you get changed and go out and do something. I have been as low as half-a-mile at a time, like after the 1974 Commonwealth Games marathon in New Zealand, when I had an injured ankle and couldn't even put my foot down. So I hopped half-a-mile. I went round the track twice in the morning, and then again in the afternoon. And for a long while I was on one-mile-a-day sessions, taking 15 minutes even to do that. You might call it bloody stupid.'

Certainly most coaches would recommend total rest for such injuries. 'Not for me though. It's just one of those things. I have to get out there and do it. I regard it as actually remedial and a measure of whether or not the injury is improving. It's my philosophy that even if I'm badly injured, I'm not going to let it get the upper hand.

'And I just don't believe anyone who says they have no time to train. I've found time for the past sixteen years, even in airports. I've always known I'd got to find fifteen minutes for a run somewhere. You have to say, "This is what I have to do, so *how* am I going to do it, and *when* am I going to do it?" '

Derek Clayton, the Australian whose controversial 2 hours 8 minutes 34 seconds run is still regarded by some authorities as having been achieved on an accurately measured course (see page 28), indicated his own tremendously punishing routine – which paved the way for his high level performances – in his book

Running to the Top. But the schedule, and his aggressive way of training, also resulted in injury, and his advice to readers was not to copy it directly.

He used a 10-week cycle to reach a peak from his normal 100 miles a week training, increasing to 120 in the first week and sometimes as much as 170 in the later stages, before easing right down in the final week. A typically heavy week went like this:

	a.m.	p.m.
Monday	7 miles easy	15 miles hard
Tuesday	7 miles easy	10 miles steady
Wednesday	7 miles easy	10–15 miles fast
Thursday	7 miles easy	15 miles fast
Friday	7 miles easy	10–12 miles easy
Saturday	22–25 miles hard	———
Sunday	17–22 miles, including hard efforts on steep hills	10 miles on racecourse

Some people would maintain that Clayton was not only aggressively dedicated, he was also self-destructive in his approach. Ron Hill's obsession with training twice a day, even if it meant hopping half a mile, also defies most medical logic. But, as Bill Adcocks maintained, if it helps to be a little mad, and if that type of obsession is a degree of madness, then its value was still shown by the fact that Clayton, Hill and Adcocks between them were running marathon-times a dozen years ago which all the additional scientific knowledge, tailor-made courses, shoe development and training refinement of recent years have not helped to significantly surpass.

Although he was not a marathon runner, Dave Bedford's own prodigious training load of up to 200 miles a week produced a world 10,000 m record, new patterns, and eventual career-destroying injury, as it did with Clayton and Adcocks. It could be that they simply reached the greatest training load their bodies could withstand, and went beyond it.

But that determination to get the training done, whatever the circumstances, usually separates the runners who have a good chance of marathon success from those who do not.

Although his career was interrupted by injury, Trevor Wright has been one of our most durable marathon performers, from his silver medal in 2:14.00 at the 1971 European championships at the age of 24, and including his third place in the 1981 London

Staying cool. *Above:* runners wait in the shade before the race.
Below: they make use of a sponging station

Heat and dehydration are the marathoner's enemies: for the novice,
it's worth taking time to ensure a proper fluid intake (*below*)

Two less orthodox but equally effective methods in the New York Marathon
of keeping down the body temperature on a hot day

Three British ladies who have made their marathon mark:

Left: Gillian Adams-Horovitz, running here in the London Marathon, was coached by the author to a UK record in 1979 and finished second in the 1980 New York Marathon

Below left: The inexhaustible Leslie Watson, who has completed over sixty marathons, and in 1981 broke the world best for 50 miles

Below: The ever-smiling Madge Sharples, at sixty-two one of the personalities of the 1981 London Marathon

Right: Two of Britain's most successful marathoners, Ron Hill (*left*) and Trevor Wright

Below: Mother of two Joyce Smith, snatching a personal drink, was the third woman to break 2½ hours, at the age of forty-three!

Below right: Ian Thompson (no. 22) leading the 1974 Commonwealth Games marathon, which he astonishingly won from super-veteran Jack Foster (no. 50)

Facing page: Down the field in the marathons at London (*left*) and New York (*right*), the distance is still the same as upfront, where Dick Beardsley and Inge Simonsen are seen sharing the 1981 London title (*below*)

Aftermath — 1. Time to reflect or collapse (*above*), or simply to check the feet for blister damage (*below*)

Aftermath — 2. A foil 'space blanket', or the more conventional type, and a drink help the body to return to normal afterwards. It's all over. Until next time

Marathon. As the first Briton home there, he clocked 2:12.53, less than half a minute outside his best time.

'In 1971 I used to run only about 70–80 miles a week in training, but I've found as I got older that I had to do more mileage. I now cover about 100–110 miles a week when I'm preparing for a marathon, starting the week with 20–25 miles on a Sunday at a steady pace.

'On Monday I do just one session of 12 miles, but include some quicker stretches, like eight times three minutes fast, then three minutes slow, during the run. On Tuesday I run the 10 miles to work, and a bit more coming back, probably 12, and I do the same on Thursdays. On Wednesday I would run just once, about 12 miles, and on Friday just six miles easy. On Saturday it's either a race or a fartlek session.

'I start easing down to 80 miles two weeks before the marathon, cutting down to one session on Tuesday and Thursday, then I really come down in the final week, and cut out the speed work too.'

Andy Holden, from Birmingham's Tipton Harriers, is perhaps one of Britain's most underrated and consistent runners, having, within ten years, been a UK record-holder and 1972 Olympic representative at the 3000-metre steeplechase, a regular cross country international, very narrowly missing the 1980 Olympic team as a marathon runner, winning the Bermuda Marathon for three consecutive years (1979–81) and setting a course record of 3:21.46 on a venture into ultra-marathoning in winning the 36¼-mile Two Bridges race from Dunfermline to Rosyth in 1980.

'In winter I run about 140 miles a week, including a couple of sessions of fast running, and a regular 25-miler on Sunday mornings at a slow pace. But it's not so much what I'm doing now as the fact that I've been running for fifteen years, and during much of that time I was doing 100 miles a week for cross country training.

'Before a marathon, I lower it from 140 for two or three weeks, and do more fast one-mile repetitions on the road, running a mile flat out, then a mile steady, alternately. On three days a week I run 6 miles to and from work, and on one of those days I meet John Graham for a lunchtime 15 mile run. It's crucial, because it's hard to go out and do 15 on your own during the week. On the other two days, I run 14 miles each way to and from work, and on Saturdays I usually run on the morning of a club race, just out of habit.'

An example of how different training patterns suit different top-class runners was clear at the 1981 AAA Marathon on the challenging Rugby course. It was won by Liverpool runner Hugh Jones, who knocked over four minutes off his best time with a course record of 2 hours 14 minutes 7 seconds. His preparations for the race had consisted solely of a steady 100 miles a week, with a long run of 19 miles on Sunday mornings, and twice-a-day steady runs of 5 miles in the morning and 8–10 in the evening, easing down to weekly totals of 70 and 55 in the fortnight before the race. He included no speed work.

Andy Holden, with his considerably higher training mileage, was second in 2:16.04, less than a minute outside his best, while third, in a personal record of 2:16.40, was Mike Gratton from Canterbury, who had recently switched from covering up to 140 miles a week to a maximum of 100, but involving a much greater proportion of quality work. It included fartlek on Tuesdays, repetition runs over 600 or 1000 m on Thursdays, and a session of alternate 5-minute fast, 6-minute jog, runs on a Saturday if he was not racing.

Gratton also did the carbohydrate loading diet for the race fairly seriously, while Holden decided against it this time because he had a cold and did not want to bring himself down physically any further, and Jones had made an attempt at following the diet, but confessed that he didn't think he had done it correctly!

Whatever specific training methods are used, there are no shortcuts. Even athletes who have been running internationally for years have discovered, when they moved up to the marathon after successful careers as track runners, that there were unsuspected pitfalls. Bernie Ford, from Feltham, who was 8th in the 1976 Olympic 10,000 metres and one of Britain's most highly consistent cross-country and road runners, decided to move up to the marathon in 1979.

Basically there is little difference between training for the marathon and the 10,000 metres, because speed is still important in the long event. The fact that Craig Virgin of the USA could run a 2:10.26 marathon at Boston just a few weeks after retaining the World Cross-Country title in 1981, proved it.

No, the difficulty arises from the way you run the race. If you're a track or road runner, then you are conditioned to cover every break in a race, to respond to every change of pace, and to always follow the leaders. But in a marathon you have to run very much your own race, know what you have to do, and stick to it. If you've a schedule worked out for a 2:10 run, and someone else sets off at 2:07 pace, he's either uncatchable, or he's eventually going to blow up. You have to stick to your guns.

In my first marathon, which was the AAA Championship at Coventry in May 1979, I found it very easy for 15–16 miles, and I was holding back. But I never knew that any race could be transformed so quickly. One minute it was unbelievably easy, the next unbelievably difficult.

At 20 miles I was beginning to suffer, and the last 6 were the longest I'd ever run. I had to make a conscious effort just to pick up the left leg, put it down, pick up the right leg, put it down, and so on.

Ford finished second to Greg Hannon in 2:14.15 on that debut, in stiflingly hot conditions.

After that, I thought, well, there's more to this game than meets the eye, because it always appears to track runners and 10-mile specialists that it's easy to get round a marathon. It *is* easy to get round, but it depends how fast you go. In those last 5–6 miles, it all starts to happen! That first race really brought it home to me, so I prepared more carefully for the next one, which was the Fukuoka classic in Japan. For that race I was doing two long runs a week, 20 miles on Sunday and 15 on Wednesday, also a bit more overall mileage, but keeping some reasonable speed there too. I started preparing for that December race in September, and during October and November I was running 120 miles a week. You can probably run a reasonable marathon off 100 miles a week if the balance of speed and steady running is right, but you must get in at least one 2-hour run each week.

Before the race, apart from a gradual taper-down, I don't do anything else special. It's not as essential to feel really sharp before a marathon as it is before a track race, because no-one is going to blast off from the very start. Or if they do, they won't last. What is important is that you are confident you have done the work, and tapered off.

In that Fukuoka race, Ford was fourth in 2:10.51, less than 100 yards behind the winner, despite falling during the race. It was the fastest marathon time by a British runner for five years, and only Ian Thompson, Ron Hill and Bill Adcocks had ever run faster among Britons.

As a result of that performance Ford was eventually picked for the 1980 Olympic Games, where it all went wrong for him. He dropped out around halfway, and again had to reappraise the event.

'I've a lot more respect for it now. But you can be your own worst enemy sometimes. Any fit athlete can run a marathon. But the emphasis has shifted more to international-level times, when perhaps we should be running a lot more domestic races in 2:18 or 2:20 to build up some experience.

'I used to think that you just came out for the really top races, two or three a year, ran very fast times, and that was it. But I'm beginning to think that you should serve an apprenticeship first. If you look at Waldemar Cierpinski, he had lots of low-key marathons, where you can experiment with your drinks and your diet, before he won the Olympics. In that way you can just run the 26 miles to get the confidence and the feel of the distance, instead of trying to run sub-2:15 straight away.'

The one material item for which any of the world's fastest runners would surely swap their records, though, is an Olympic gold medal. And the man who won the marathon at the last two Olympic Games, Waldemar Cierpinski of East Germany, revealed after his 1980 win in Moscow that he had worked on a three-year plan for that one race. 'Every day, almost every minute was leading up to that day, to the 2 hours 11 minutes it took me to cover the Olympic course. I did not particularly care about my results in the meantime. I just lived and trained according to plan.

'It takes a marathon man a long time to prepare thoroughly, both physically and theoretically. Physically, there was no question that I had to be fit. But we also worked out all variants and options theoretically. I busied myself with theoretical studies at the German Association of Physical Culture, delving into questions of methodology, and the reactions of the body under stress, so that in Moscow I could reach back into that store of theoretical projections and analyses, and fortify my spirit with knowledge already digested.'

It is hard to imagine many of Britain's leading runners taking it quite to that extreme, but the fact remains that Cierpinski has won twice in Olympic marathons, and no one from Britain has ever done so. In fact, while Cierpinski was winning that second title in Moscow, Britain was enduring a particularly black day as none of the three UK runners finished the race. And while Cierpinski had been putting the finishing touches to his three-year plan, and already knew long before that he was going to launch his attack precisely at the 35-kilometre mark in the Moscow event, Britain's trio of runners were actually chosen less than three months before the race.

Peaking, especially in an event with special demands like the

marathon, is never more important than in the Olympics; there is
no second chance. But in some way the great strength of British
distance running is also its prime weakness. While Cierpinski was
far and away the best marathon runner in East Germany, knew he
was going to Moscow a very long time beforehand, and was their
only Olympic competitor in the race, the British selectors were
faced with at least a dozen potential Olympians before the final
selection race, the 1980 AAA Championships race in early May,
with the Olympic event on 1 August.

Consequently, most of the British runners knew that they were
going to have to be at peak fitness in early May, because if they
were not, they simply would not make the team in the face of such
strong opposition. It would be pointless to be in excellent fettle on
1 August, while sitting at home watching it on TV.

So the May date became an even more important focus during
the winter months of preparation, because you couldn't succeed
in the second race unless you succeeded in the first. In fact, the one
runner who chose to miss the trial (which was not compulsory,
but the major factor for selection) was Bernie Ford, who 'sat' on
his 2:10.51 performance in Japan the previous December.

In that AAA race, on a blustery day and a twisting, narrow
course, not even the winner Ian Thompson (2:14.00) or runner-
up Dave Black (2:14.28) came near Ford's time. The selectors
subsequently chose Thompson, Black and Ford, missing out the
third man in that AAA race, Andy Holden, who had run a
personal best of 2:15.18, despite losing some time because of a call
of nature during the race.

The fact that Ford had not had to race a marathon between
December and August still proved of little advantage, in fact,
because it was not until after the May trial that he was finally
certain he was going to Moscow. Choosing to sit it out also had an
adverse effect on his training, which may be worth noting for any
athlete in the same position in future.

'Although I hadn't been picked officially for Moscow, I knew
before the AAA race that things were stacked in my favour. But I
think I still felt subconsciously obligated to be training very hard
at the time of the trial, even though I wasn't considering doing it.
I'm sure that at that time I could actually have run a very good
marathon.

'But the whole point of missing the race was *not* to be at my
fittest at that time. Yet when it came to the Olympic race I was

probably already over the top. I'd had a period of 2–3 weeks at only 90 miles a week, when I felt I'd lost my edge, then a month before the Games I suddenly picked up again and I was trying very hard to make up for lost time.

'So up to the week before the race in Moscow, when I should have been tapering down, I was still training very hard, and on the day I just felt very, very sluggish.'

There may be lessons to learn from Ford's experience. Why, for instance, did he feel 'subconsciously obligated' to be training very hard at the time of the trial? Could it have been, as I suspect, from the weight of opinion of his closest rivals that he, too, should run the AAA race?

Selection is always going to be a problem. On the one hand, with so many runners challenging for a place, a trial race would seem to be the only fair way of selecting the maximum of three runners allowed per country in the Olympics. That trial has to be close enough to the Games to show who is in form, but not so close that recovery before the Olumpic race is impossible for a new peak to be realistically planned. It worked for Frank Shorter in 1972, on the US cut-throat system of the first three in their Olympic Trial being selected. He went on to win the gold medal in Munich.

But four years later he was defeated in the Montreal Olympics by Waldemar Cierpinski, whom we now know may plan specifically for up to three years before the Olympics, not three months. The Americans, in turn, have what could be seen as an advantage in one sense in always sticking to their trials 'first three go' policy, with no arguments or special cases.

In Britain we tend to stick to picking the marathon trio some three months before the Olympics, based mainly on a trial, but not exclusively. Special cases, fast times abroad, and sudden illnesses are all considered too. The resulting selection rarely satisfies everybody, particularly those runners who have been trying to take out the insurance of a fast race abroad.

An alternative selection method could be to pick a British athlete sufficiently far in advance – say one year – for him to be able to plan fully for just one peak that Olympic season. But then you hit another selectorial problem. What criteria should you adopt for such a selection to be made? There are enough international marathons around for the top athletes to continue to race, yet avoid meeting each other if they wish. To select by performance alone, with so many course and climate differences, is always a controversial action. What happens if someone runs 1:58 down the side of Mount Everest?

An outstanding recent competitive record in international championships might suffice. I always thought that Ian Thompson should have been selected for the 1976 Montreal Olympic team without a trial, as reigning European and Commonwealth champion. He was also holder of the world's second-fastest ever time, which itself had been achieved in a major Games in 1974 on a flat, accurately measured course. But Thompson ran no marathons in 1975, was made to run the AAA race in May 1976 to prove his form, and finished 7th. 'Told you so' said those who wanted him to run in the trial. But it still did not prove to me that he would not have finished higher than the leading British marathon runner in those Games, who was 26th.

Ron Hill's chances of winning in 1972 were not helped by having to run a trial race which he resented, and though he safely made the Olympic team, his disappointing Olympic 6th place in Munich was probably only partly caused by the unexpected effects of altitude training just before the Games.

To be fair, let's look at the other side of the coin too, though. Suppose the British selectors actually decided to plump for selecting a (mythical) runner, Jimmy Goldenboots, a full year before the Olympics.

'Okay, Jimmy,' they tell him. 'You're in. Do what you want to prepare. See you in Los Angeles.'

A possible public reaction would be, 'Blimey, if they've selected Jimmy Goldenboots now, they must reckon he's a cert for the gold.' And all Jimmy hears for a year is 'Off to get that gold yet then, Jim?'

But immediate reaction among some of his rival British athletes could be, 'Blimey, now we're running for two places, instead of three, and three was bad enough. How do we know he's going to still be that fit next year? He ought to run the trial with the rest of us to show he's still in shape.' So there is a danger that instead of support in his own country, Jimmy just senses jealousy, envy, and accusations of favouritism, and imagines that a great many people want him to do badly in the Games.

As he tries to prepare quietly, any time he shows his face at a race everyone else tries like hell to beat him just because he's Jimmy Goldenboots, the Selected Olympic Athlete. So either he has to try to run brilliantly all year defeating all-comers, instead of concentrating on training, or he has to shrug off defeats by lesser athletes, confident (or trying to be confident) that it will all turn out right on the big day. Meanwhile there is loud dressing-room talk that 'Jimmy Goldenboots didn't look so good today, did he? I wonder if they'll drop him from the Olympic team now?'

Alternatively, he can just avoid any races of a significant distance, which could be detrimental to his preparation anyway. And at the end of it all, the expectation will be that after all that special treatment, he'd better damn well produce the goods. . . .

All right, so that is taking the most pessimistic, cynical view. But understandably international athletes tend to be very sensitive about anyone else getting any help, advantage or 'favours' of which they felt they did not have a chance themselves.

The circumstances leading up to the 1984 Olympic Games might just allow a selection situation which has not been tried before. If, from the results of the 1982 European and Commonwealth Games marathons, a single outstanding British male and female athlete could be selected, they could be named straight-away then for the 1983 inaugural World Championships in Helsinki.

That would give each of them nearly a year of 'dress rehearsal' for the pressures of preparing for one major race, and a chance to make mistakes and rectify them. With that initial selection would go a promise that *if* the runner were to be the first British competitor home in the World Championships, then he or she would automatically be selected for the Los Angeles Olympics, with a further year to prepare.

If a selected athlete is not the first Briton home in Helsinki, for whatever reason, then he will have to earn his place for Los Angeles like everyone else. The other British representatives for Helsinki and Los Angeles would still be selected in the normal way, to ensure everyone had a chance of making the team.

By establishing such a clear procedure, the British selectors could create a situation unprecedented at least in recent years. They would say: 'Do well in that race, and we will select you for the Olympics a year in advance.'

If they do that, every one has two possible routes to the Olympic gold medal. And if they fail they will only be able to offer by way of an explanation: 'I didn't run fast enough.'

5

Clothes and Climate

Nothing can replace training pure and simple if you want to run the marathon faster, but there is no doubt that looking smart and feeling comfortable in a race can give you a little psychological 'lift'. Yet looking smart and feeling comfortable are not, of course, necessarily the same thing. An elegant lady attending Royal Ascot may be dressed immaculately, but if it starts to pour with rain and she has to run, or rather totter, on her high heels for shelter, with one hand holding on to her hat, then smartness counts for naught in practical terms.

And a marathon runner has to be practical above all else. Your shoes, or shorts, or vest may seem comfortable in a shop, or on a short training run, but what will they be like when soaked with sweat, or rain, after several hours' running.

The first rule, therefore, is never to start a marathon wearing any item of clothing that you haven't thoroughly tested before in long runs. Especially shoes, for there are few more frustrating experiences than having to drop out of a race for which you have prepared long and hard, not because of any excessive fatigue in your body but simply because your shoes have blistered your feet so badly.

You may take 25,000 to 30,000 strides in an average marathon, but if by halfway your toes are rubbed raw, or your shorts are chafing your legs, you are not going to enjoy the experience very much. And the marathon is quite hard enough already without introducing other little distractions on the debit side. So decide at least three weeks in advance what you intend to wear for a particular race, and then methodically test each item during your longest training runs.

Your new 'Zokko Pheidippides PB84' shoes may look terrific, but if they turn your toenails black in 10 miles they are really not a great deal of use to you for marathon running.

Shoes

Surprisingly perhaps, experienced international athletes still, from time to time, find out the hard way that you cannot get away with wearing brand new shoes for a marathon. Usually they have been track runners moving up in distance, and who had suffered no damage previously when wearing new shoes in a 10,000-metre track race, or even a 10-mile road event. But the marathon, you will not need reminding, is different.

One culprit in this is the development of the road running shoe itself. The nylon which, since the late sixties, has almost completely replaced the heavier, less pliable leather in the manufacture of shoe uppers and certainly breaks in more quickly, is lighter in weight and dries more easily. But even nylon shoes have to be stitched together in places, and if they are made on a last which does not resemble your feet, then they will probably be engaged in some form of disagreement with your feet on every one of those 25,000–30,000 strides.

Whenever possible, you should buy running shoes in person rather than by mail, trying on both shoes together, properly laced up, and walk (or if possible jog) around the shop in them, looking for any warning signs of tightness or cramping in the toes.

Don't be afraid to try on a dozen different pairs, and then not buy any of them, because they are expensive items, and you must be sure they will suit you. I once bought a pair of gold-coloured lightweight road shoes, even though they were 1½ sizes too big for me, because the shop did not have any smaller ones in stock. I still don't know why I did it, but every other day for two months I'd try them on in case my feet had unexpectedly grown. Then, when I realized they weren't going to, I had to sell them for about half what I paid for them. A fruitless, expensive, illogical exercise.

Examine all aspects of the shoes closely, and particularly the thickness of the heel. The distance runner lands heavily on the heel on practically every stride taken, and it has to be substantial enough to cushion the shock of around eighty percent of the body weight landing on an unyielding surface like pavement or road. Many shoes have a heel wedge – an extra layer of rubber between the midsole and sole – but the overall thickness of the heel must not be so great that your weight is thrown too far forward, making it feel as though you are constantly running downhill.

To have too thick a heel also reduces the force exerted by the

Achilles tendon on each stride. So a happy medium is usually the answer; personally I prefer shoes with a heel about ¾ inch thick.

The heel also has to be wide enough to prevent instability, and some road shoes now have a 'flared' heel, in which the sole actually widens towards the ground. This also helps to spread the load of shock, but some runners with a particular gait complain that the edge of a flared sole can cause cuts on the opposite leg if the foot knocks it.

A heel counter is the reinforced section curving around the angle and often covered with suede, which stabilizes the heel on landing. But the heel tab above it is a controversial aspect on many running shoes. It is the hump which rises on the back of the shoe, above the heel counter, and exists ostensibly to protect the Achilles tendon, and also in pulling on the shoe. Some doctors, however, insist that a rigid heel tab can itself cause Achilles tendon problems by digging into the vulnerable base of the tendon on every stride.

Built-in arch supports are another grey area. Theoretically, they should help, but evidence from the USA has suggested that although they may feel comfortable, they actually offer no bio-mechanical assistance for most runners. Remember that the manufacturers are turning out millions of pairs of running shoes made on lasts which are designed to represent the average foot. In fact, relatively few people actually have an 'average' foot. Most feet are as different as our finger prints, and one estimation is that arch supports actually suit no more than 10 percent of the buyers of running shoes, and the rest are better off without them. In the USA the trend is towards 'orthotics', which are plastic shoe inserts, often custom-made, to correct any foot problems.

The sole of a running shoe needs the best of both worlds. It must be reasonably well-cushioned to protect the forefoot against too much shock, but flexible enough to allow natural foot movement, particularly at the point of maximum bend, where there is a major system of joints in the ball of the foot, which must not be restricted in movement by an over-stiff sole.

The toe-box, at the front of the shoe, should provide sufficient height and width to prevent the toes being cramped even when the feet expand, as they do when hot. One authority sensibly suggests it is better to buy running shoes late in the afternoon rather than the morning, because the feet can be slightly bigger at that time of day! Allow ¼ inch of room in front of the toes, especially if you have Morton's Foot, a condition in which the second toe is longer than the big toe. Running in shoes which are too tight, particularly going downhill, is like kicking a brick wall.

Padding around the ankle, the cushioned rim featured by some shoes, helps to prevent those blisters which are often caused in cheaper shoes by having little more than the thickness of the shoe material (and sometimes an irritating seam) around the ankle.

'Breaking in' is an important process, even for shoes that fit well. They need to adapt to the exact movements of the joints in your feet, and the best way is to wear them around the house for a few days, and jog a couple of miles in them, before using them for training or racing – and even then start off using them only for shorter distances.

If you live in an area where you cannot easily get to a sports shop with a range of different shoes, ask as many other runners as you can which shoes they wear, and what they think of them. Don't just believe the advertising blurb: of course the manufacturers are going to tell you that every one of their shoes is just what you've been waiting for. If you have to order by post, send an outline of your foot with your order, because sizes differ slightly between manufacturers, and it may save you having to return the shoes later if they don't fit. But if they still don't fit, don't be afraid to send them back. It is better to wait an extra few days for the right-sized shoes than to run for six months in the wrong ones.

The weight of shoes is again a matter of personal preference. Very light road racing shoes (often made on the same type of last as spiked track racing shoes) are available, but to attempt to cover high training mileages in such shoes would probably lead to injury. They are simply not substantial enough to protect the feet from the constant pounding every day, and there is a growing feeling in the USA, as a result of the considerable research undertaken during the running boom of the last decade, that the lightest shoes are probably only of benefit to the fastest 10 percent of marathon runners.

The American podiatrist Dr Steven Subotnick has expressed the opinion that unless you are going to run a marathon at a speed faster than 5½-minutes-a-mile pace (2 hours 24 minutes 12 seconds pace), then you should be content to wear a good training shoe rather than a light racing model because otherwise, as your running form deteriorates in the last 10 miles of a slower marathon, your joints, muscles and skeleton have to absorb more stress and need greater shock absorption in the shoes.

Figures presented to the American College of Sports Medicine have demonstrated that the amount of extra energy expended by marathon runners wearing training shoes instead of the lighter shoes was only three percent, whereas the heavier shoes in turn offered twenty-five percent more shock absorption.

Protecting the legs from the considerable shock is one of the main functions of running shoes anyway, together with motion control (to stop the foot rolling too much inwards or outwards) and traction. For a time, in the quest for maximum shock absorption, some road shoes became too soft in the sole which resulted in a number of leg injuries, which they were trying to prevent. Now the designs are reaching a happy medium.

I am constantly being asked which model of shoes is the best, but unlike the date of the Battle of Hastings, there is no precise answer. If there were, all the other shoe companies would go out of business. Different shoes suit different feet, and the only real solution is to jump in – with both feet! – and try to find which particular model is most suited to you. But don't forget that those shoes should carry you for thousands of miles, so it is worth spending more than five minutes in finding them.

Socks

Socks help to reduce the blister-causing friction between your foot and the inside of your shoe, to absorb sweat, and to help cut down shock as your foot hits the road. For long training runs, there can be a certain psychological reassurance about having thick socks with reinforced soles, but in races some runners prefer thin, lightweight socks, or no socks at all. The same rule should apply as for shoes though: don't wait for the race itself to try out running in thinner socks or no socks; try it in a training run first.

The socks should always be clean, because dried 'sweaty' socks can have sharp crinkles in them which may then cause the very blisters they are supposed to prevent. The same applies to darns; if a sock has a hole in it, throw it out, or at least don't run in it. Cotton or wool absorbs moisture better than nylon, which dries quicker but can be uncomfortable in hot weather.

If you do choose to run without socks, which some runners find cooler and psychologically lighter, rub Vaseline on parts of the foot which may be susceptible to blistering, particularly the prime areas, like the tops of the toes and around the heel. Some runners put a thin piece of sponge between their heel and the inside of the back of the shoe. Even if you get away without taking any of these precautions in training, remember that in a race you will be running for longer, and with greater intensity, than in training.

Shorts

Men's shorts should be brief cut but airy, not too tight at the waist, but comfortably secure. Although cotton is more absorbent, nylon shorts are now more popular, being light and quick to dry. The range of movement afforded by the shorts should be considerable, without being indecent; sawn off jeans are not very practical! Some of the latest shorts have a built-in supporter, and ordinary pants or swimming trunks are now widely preferred to the jockstrap.

For girls, the style of square-cut looser nylon shorts already popular among female runners in the USA are now more widely in evidence among Britain's leading marathon runners, although the towelling, briefer cut, elasticated design, which is otherwise virtually standard in track events, is still widely used too. The pants worn under either should be cotton rather than nylon for its greater absorbency.

Vests

Club athletes, often restricted in their choice of vest for shorter races because of the rules relating to wearing club colours in certain events, have more of a free hand in road races above 20 kilometres (12½ miles), where the AAA Rules state that for races of that distance or above 'clubs may nominate alternative light-coloured vests, including white, with a club badge'.

This relatively recent modification came about because it was accepted that light colours reflect the sun's rays while dark colours absorb more of them. In a long race on a hot day, an athlete who had to compete in his club's dark colours would be at a disadvantage over another whose club had white colours.

Vests should not be too tight, particularly under the arms, and on cold days long-sleeved vests are sometimes worn under, or instead of, the more conventional style.

On warmer days mesh or string vests have now become almost standard wear among many of the leading male marathoners, as they help to dissipate the body's heat. Unfortunately, they have also brought about an increase in the incidence of a complaint quaintly known as 'jogger's nipple', as the sawing action of the mesh vest during the race causes a soreness, or even bleeding, which can be prevented by covering the nipples with sticking plaster, or smearing with Vaseline, beforehand.

There are now special marathon vests on the market which incorporate a standard top half, usually nylon, with a mesh 'midriff', which is also an acceptable model for female marathon runners. However, for the less ambitious, who will not be running at such a fast pace, nor producing so much body heat, a comfortable standard tee-shirt will usually be quite adequate.

Tracksuits

Most runners eventually accumulate a wardrobe full of clothes designated their 'training gear'. It may include tracksuits, tee-shirts, anoraks, slop-shirts, and so on, bought from an athletics specialist shop, or it may just consist of a number of comfortable garments which started off as everyday wear. How much you spend on a tracksuit, for example, is very much a question of personal preference. It could be a smart, well-cut, fleecy-lined model, or just a cheap version from the nearest chain store. Both will function equally well.

But avoid suits which have baggy or flared trousers. In 'baggies', with a strong wind against you, you'll not only block the pavement, but your legs will feel as cold as if they were in the open air. And with flared trousers, they will feel the same, at least from the kneecaps down, as a Force Eight blast freezes your calves. Whoever designed flared tracksuit trousers didn't realize how impractical they are for either running, or simply for keeping warm on a cold, windy day.

Any variety of top will normally substitute for a tracksuit top, although a series of thin layers is better than one thick layer. And beware of woollen jumpers on a wet day; you can end up virtually treading on the sleeves when they start absorbing rain. But there are few substitutes for tracksuit trousers for comfort and range of movement, either for warming up or training, or even (for the modest performer) racing.

Bras

During their running boom the Americans, thorough to the last, have even researched 'the motion of the female breasts during athletic activity', and results given to the US publication *Running Times* by doctors – female doctors, I hasten to add – from the New Jersey Medical School and the University of Oklahoma, concluded that the breasts are vulnerable to damage if not properly supported. A normal 'fashion' bra is unsuitable for running, being too elastic, shiny, non-absorbent and too flimsy, with a tendency to ride up and for the shoulder straps to slip off.

A number of manufacturers have now produced special sports bras which feature a non-abrasive fabric, a mostly non-elastic material ('in order to minimize motion of the breasts relative to the body'), wide straps forming a 'V' or cross at the back to prevent slipping, and no exposed hardware to dig into the skin.

There is even a Jogbra invented by two American women runners, who explained that they had studied a jockstrap rather than other bras. 'We cut two jockstraps in half, sewed them together,' one explained, 'and they kept us from bouncing.' There seems little one can add to that.

Adapting to the Conditions

Two people looked out of their windows on the same summer morning and saw clear blue skies and a bright sun. One said: 'What a marvellous day!' The other groaned to himself, and sat down to think about the problems it would cause. Which one was the marathon runner?

Two people looked out of the window and saw a grey, cheerless day, with a light rain spattering the window panes. One groaned to himself, and cancelled his plans for that morning. The other said nothing, but felt a surge of adrenalin in the face of such weather conditions. Which one was the marathon runner?

When all the training has been done, every last preparation made, the one factor over which you have no control is the climate, which in Britain seems to become more and more unpredictable. In the past couple of years I've watched midwinter cross country races in warm sunshine, and competed on the track in May in snow! In an event lasting as long as the marathon, conditions may even change radically between start and finish; but generally you can tell how it is likely to affect the race.

Heat

Of all the different conditions you meet, heat is the most difficult with which to deal, because you cannot escape from it, like wearing extra layers in the cold or sheltering behind someone else in the wind. You can only try to minimize its effects. The most serious of these is the threat of dehydration, the loss of water through sweating, which in turn leads to a rise in body temperature. A great proportion of blood is sent to the skin surface for cooling during such exercises as marathon running, which in turn means that less is available for powering the muscles, so cooling the body is of prime importance.

Sweating, in which the sweat glands send to the skin surface fluid which evaporates, cooling the skin surface as it does so, is one of nature's methods. But if the air is high in humidity, and especially if there is a following wind, the sweat does not evaporate easily and its cooling effectiveness is reduced. Meanwhile the body temperature remains high and dehydration from continued sweat loss threatens.

Convection occurs when a slight headwind, which is increased by the effect of the athlete running, also helps to cool the body naturally (sweating increases when you stop running and the convection ceases). But artificial methods of cooling during the race are also essential.

Sopping wet sponges are offered to athletes at regular intervals in long road races, and on a hot day you should use them to wipe the face, neck, shoulders and thighs as priority, squeezing some of the water over your head too. Sucking the sponge to take in fluid is not particularly recommended because of the dubious contents of a sponge when it has been tossed down the roadside after use. The sponges are usually plunged back into buckets of water, which in turn eventually become somewhat gritty, and I have likened the use of one of these to wiping your face with a Brillo pad.

But unless you are in urgent need of fluid, the refreshment stations should be sufficient to provide for your liquid needs. It is advisable to take drinks well before you feel the need, and on hot days the earlier the better, to avoid the onset of dehydration. In its extreme form, a vicious circle can occur whereby, through a continuation of hard exercise, the flow of blood to the skin surface is eventually reduced and diverted back to assist with the powering of the muscles. The sweat rate subsequently increases, dehydration looms more seriously as a result of the sweating, there is further reduction in the flow of blood to the skin, so the body temperature rises again, the sweat rate increases, and so on. The eventual outcome of this chain, known as the hyperthermic spiral,

would be heat-stroke unless you eased down the pace considerably, cooled off, or took a drink.

Runners may lose seven pints of sweat in a race, depending on
conditions, and it has to be made up quickly. Pure cold water is
absorbed rapidly, and even glucose added to it can reduce the
speed of its absorption. Solids should be avoided during a
marathon, because they can delay the absorption of liquids too, as
well as using up energy in being absorbed themselves, and cannot
usefully contribute to energy supplies quickly anyway.

The drinks provided at refreshment stations for all competitors
in marathon races in Britain usually consist of paper cups of
orange or lemon squash, water, and sometimes cold tea.
Additionally, in most races you can hand in your 'personal' drinks
to officials beforehand. The relevant AAA Rules 107 (f) state:

'In Marathon races refreshments shall be provided by the
organizers at approximately 3 miles (5 Km) and thereafter at
approximately every 3 miles (5 Km). In addition the organizers
shall provide sponging stations where water only shall be supplied
approximately midway between refreshment stations.

'No refreshment may be carried or taken by a competitor other
than that provided by the organizers: a competitor may submit to
the organizers any special type of refreshment required and this, if
approved, must then be handed to the organizers at a time and
place specified by them and shall be available at the refreshment
stations nominated by the competitor.'

These personal drinks, of your own concoction, should ideally be
in plastic bottles and must be clearly marked with your race
number. A method of collection is usually in operation at the
dressing rooms, where a series of cardboard boxes is set out, one
for each refreshment station along the route. You simply leave
your drinks in the relevant boxes, and the officials transport them
out on the course; give yourself plenty of time to do so, however, as
the boxes are sometimes taken out well before the start.

In the best-organized races you will find the personal drinks
placed on the tables before the 'mass' drinks. That way, if an
athlete misses his personal drink, there is still time to grab a cup of
something else without going back. Some races, however, put the
personal drinks after the mass drinks.

Ordinary screw-top plastic bottles can be used for these personal drinks, but the most practical type are those with some
simple mechanism for squirting the fluid into your mouth, rather

than requiring you to suck, which is difficult when trying to maintain your breathing pattern. Suitable bottles designed specifically for hair sprays can be bought (unused!) quite cheaply, although the spray hole may have to be considerably enlarged to ensure a full jet of liquid. There are also specially manufactured feeding bottles with a plastic straw, which are a vast improvement on the home-made version I once used which took me so long to charge into action that I might just as well have used an ordinary paper cup.

Bill Rodgers has been known to actually stop in the Boston Marathon to ensure he took in all of his drink (and still won), while Ian Thompson puts his hand over the top of the cup to gain some control over the contents on the run, before attempting to drink. Otherwise the contents would shoot out at his 5-minute-mile pace.

The concept of personal drinks is a good one for a reasonably compact field, but for the mass marathons, like London and New York, impossible to organize. In these big events, some runners do arrange for friends in the crowd to hand them personal drinks at prearranged points on the course, and in New York, Boston, and many other US races, crowds offer drinks to runners along much of the route. Children, particularly, are delighted if a runner accepts the cup they are holding out, and this brief Samaritan act between two people who will never meet each other for more than a fleeting second adds to the community spirit of the whole race.

Others set up fine sprays with garden hoses to cool down runners on hot days, and at the Montreal Marathon special frames, like doorways, were set up by the organizers around the course with a spray on top through which the runners could decide whether or not to run. In Boston there is not always the choice at some of the narrower parts, but the spray is normally welcome and refreshing to the runners. Only occasionally, like the time a well-meaning bystander threw a bucket of icy water over an unsuspecting runner, immediately causing both of his thighs to cramp up, has such help been positively unwelcome.

Strictly speaking, the passing of drinks and other aid must be considered as contravening the rules, as the IAAF Rules are the same in essence as those in Britain, while adding: 'A competitor taking refreshments at a place other than the refreshment points appointed by the organizers renders himself liable to disqualification.'

But it has been tacitly accepted in some major US races for years, perhaps because above all it helps protect the well-being and safety of the runners in hot conditions. At the 1980 Boston Marathon, Bill Rodgers even went on local TV the night before what was obviously going to be a very warm day and appealed to people living along the route to bring out water from their houses for the runners.

On a hot day, warm-up for the race should be restricted to a gentle jog to ensure that all kit, and especially shoes, is comfortable and that the numbers pinned to the vest will not cause any problems. Stay in the shade as much as possible, and take short drinks every few minutes to help ward off possible dehydration later. After leaving the dressing rooms for the last time, a small polythene bag of water can be used, with a small piece of sponge, to cool the neck, face and legs up to the last minute, and then handed to someone to discard carefully before the start.

Be conservative in your early pace on a hot day, erring on the side of caution of anything, and take in plenty of liquid at the earliest opportunity. After the race, when you have satisfied your immediate thirst, keep taking short drinks at 20-minute intervals, until the normal pattern of urination returns.

If at some point in the race you start to experience problems in the heat, which may include confusion of thoughts, dizziness, or shivering, you should reduce the pace, or stop altogether. Lie down in the shade, with the feet raised. Sponging down with cool water and a good intake of liquid should aid recovery, although in more serious cases, medical help may be needed. By adapting carefully to the conditions and following the guidelines it should rarely become that extreme, however.

Kit should be as light coloured as possible, and some form of white hat may be useful as long as it can 'breathe' too, and does not allow its own heat build-up. In the USA, where extremes of temperature are much greater at both ends of the scale than in Britain, runners often pin their numbers to their shorts, so that they can discard their vests if it gets too hot, and thus expose a great area of skin for heat evaporation. At a 1980 road race in Evergreen, Colorado, one female runner actually stripped off in similar fashion and finished topless. In Britain, where vests are compulsory for both male and female runners, she would have been disqualified, not to mention famous, but in the USA her action simply led the race organizer to consider whether there ought to be a special prize category for topless runners in future years.

Cold, rain and wind

For a heat-producing activity like running, a cold day is less of a problem than a hot one. Apart from sensible dressing for the weather in training, with layers of T-shirts, tracksuits and other kit according to personal preference, a woollen hat (for a third of body heat is lost through the head) and gloves or mittens may be favoured by some runners during races as well as training. Both can be discarded if you feel you are over-heating. An alternative to ordinary gloves is the fingerless variety, which help to keep your hands at a moderate temperature.

Although cold muscles perform less efficiently than warm muscles, the well-protected heart actually works more easily in cold weather, because it does not have to continually pump blood to the skin surface for cooling, as it does in hot weather. Additionally, fewer calories per mile are burned. Dr Frank Consolazio of the Letterman Army Institute of Research in California, reviewing medical literature on calories used in heat and cold, found that there is an increase of only between 2 and 5 per cent in energy-utilization in extremely cold weather, which can be attributed entirely to the effect of having to wear extra layers of clothing. In cold weather, energy requirements are otherwise dependent simply on bodyweight and intensity of exercise. But in exceptionally hot weather there is an estimated increase in energy requirements of 0.5 per cent for every one degree increase in temperature between 30° and 40° Centigrade, because of this need to pump blood to the skin surface for cooling.

The wind chill factor is also a consideration in the bitterest climates. This is the estimated decrease in temperature according to the strength of the prevailing wind. For example, on a day when the thermometer reads 35° Fahrenheit, a headwind of just 15 m.p.h. can turn that effectively into a temperature of only 15°.

A rain-suit jacket, even on a dry day, worn over other layers will help to take the worst of the wind off you. When training on a cold, windy day, try to set out into the wind and return with it behind you, rather than the other way round. If you start with the wind behind you, you will sweat early on, then have to run into the wind which will evaporate the sweat and make you even colder.

On the day of the race, when limbs may be exposed to the

elements, some runners like to rub olive oil, or even the type of warming massage creams used for soft tissue injuries, on to the areas of skin to be exposed as a way of trying to retain body heat.

Running in the rain can help to cool the body on a mild day, and be positively refreshing in washing away dust, salt and sweat. On other occasions, when it lashes down, it can be a curse, especially for those of us who wear glasses. The use of a long-peaked waterproof cap can often keep the worst of it from covering your spectacles (and there may be a fortune for anyone who invents a micro-chip windscreen-wiper for glasses).

Vaseline in the friction areas can be especially important on a wet day, and the nylon kit which can be so uncomfortable in hot conditions is more practical through its minimal absorbency, especially when the rain stops, as it dries off so quickly.

There are few more frustrating experiences if you want to run a particular time in a race than being caught in a vicious wind which forces you to practically run on the spot. I still remember my helpless annoyance when I competed in my first 10-miler, at Tonbridge in 1968, desperately keen to break the hour, and being brought almost to a standstill by the winds at one point. There was simply no-one who could be handily blamed! In such circumstances there is little you can do, except try to relax into the wind, almost leaning on it, and try to avoid tensing up, which will restrict your running action.

On a circuit course, you will naturally also benefit from the wind following you at some point (and at Tonbridge, which has two 5-mile laps, I eased the frustration when I was blown up a longish climb, and finished in 57.26). But they do not exactly balance out. When you run into a wind you are increasing the velocity at which it hits you. When you run with the wind, you are reducing the amount it helps you, although there is a bonus in as much as the wind allows your muscles to relax more, and work with greater efficiency.

On an A-to-B course, though, a headwind can be a disaster. It can also be a fickle friend, as runners in New Orleans know well. At the 1979 Mardi Gras Marathon there, a local police strike caused a last-minute change of course to include a 24-mile long, flat, straight, causeway over Lake Pontchartrain, which provided a strong following breeze. The winner, John Dimick of the USA, improved his best time by over 4 minutes to 2 hours 11 minutes 53 seconds, while the women's winner, Gayle Olinek, improved hers by a full quarter of an hour to a Commonwealth 'record' of 2 hours 38 minutes 12 seconds.

The organizers subsequently realized that their makeshift course could actually attract a lot of runners wanting such favourable conditions for setting a personal best time, so they adopted it as their normal route. In 1980, Ron Tabb of the US, duly set a personal best, winning in 2 hours 11 minutes and 1 second, with Olinek improving the women's course record of 2 hours 35 minutes 39 seconds. Its fame spread.

By 1981 there were no less than 2000 starters on the white concrete causeway, all confidently expecting super-fast, wind-assisted times. Alas for them, the gusts changed direction and blew at 35 m.p.h. into their faces all the way, and Doug Kurtis (who had run 2:14.16 the previous year) staggered home to win in 2:33.59, while the women's winner did just under 3:10. 'It felt like I was running uphill the whole way,' said Kurtis, and while the miserable leaders had battled the wind up front, one even threatened to throw another over the edge of the causeway if he stepped on his heels again. Now that *is* frustration.

6

Plans and Pitfalls: Food for Thought

There is no doubt that the more seriously you take the marathon, the more it dominates your life. But because it is not an event which you can throw off at frequent intervals, or with the minimum of physical effort, you owe it to yourself (and your family!) at the end of a long training regime to use every single opportunity to increase your chance of achieving a performance as near to your optimum as possible, no matter how fast or slow.

So it is worth spending a little time considering some of the external factors which could affect your run on the day, and how advance planning and attention to detail can help.

The Week Before the Race

As the day of a marathon draws nearer, so you must physically and mentally prepare to meet it. Still feeling the effects of tiredness from fatiguingly long training runs immediately before the race will not help, so in the final week training mileage should drop away to around half the normal load, with the majority of it coming early in the week. The longest run could come on the Sunday before a Saturday marathon, with another medium-length run on Wednesday, but on other days, particularly Thursday and Friday, you should do little more than jog. Remember the equation: hard work *plus rest* equals success. The last few days before a marathon are too late to do runs of sufficient length to have any positive effect on your stamina and still recover before the race.

If you decide to undertake the carbohydrate loading diet, which is explained more fully later in this chapter, then Sunday will be the occasion for your long 'glycogen bleed-out' run, and Wednesday lunchtime will be a high point of your week as you switch to stuffing yourself with carbohydrates. But for a first time marathoner, that type of diet is best left alone.

The final few days are simply a time to conserve energy, to be a little lazy, and catch up on some of that reading you have been meaning to do, all those letters you should have written, and finally seeing the films everyone else is talking about. And as you ease off training, so you should feel a little more lively than usual, and going out for a walk to burn up a little excess nervous energy won't hurt.

Everyone has their own way of relaxing. Some might prefer early nights in the final week, which is fine as long as you can sleep, and not spend the extra time restlessly. Others may find that going to bed a little later than usual may help them to get off to sleep more quickly.

This is the period when you should check on details for the race. Are you absolutely sure you have got the date and the starting time right? Check your official instructions, which will have been sent in acknowledgement of your entry. What do you mean, you haven't had an acknowledgement of your entry? Check with the organizers straight away to ensure they received it; don't leave it until the day of the race, when it may cost you valuable energy.

Are you sure you know exactly where the changing rooms and the start are? You won't want to waste energy on the day walking miles looking for them.

If you are travelling to the race by public transport, inquire in advance about train or bus times, and make sure they give you sufficient breathing space before the race to go through all the pre-race preparations without rushing them. It is better to arrive half an hour early than ten minutes late. Have you checked for the possibility of weekend railway engineering works on the route you are using, which will not be shown in timetables, but could delay you? If you're going by car, does the driver (if it's not you, or even if it is) know the best route, and how long it will take?

All these things may seem trivial, obvious items. But when your mind is on the race itself, they can be overlooked, and the one thing you want on the day of the event is the absolute minimum of unnecessary hassle. You want to get to the venue as quickly and smoothly as possible, to concentrate on the race, and not to have to worry overmuch on the day about fringe details, like travel.

Sometimes, if a long journey is involved, you may need to stay overnight beforehand. If so, try to stay away from town centres, which can be noisy places, especially on Friday and Saturday nights when the pubs empty. Choose the best accommodation you can afford, because after the months and months of training, for whatever level of result you are aiming, you will not want to undermine your chances at the eleventh hour by sacrificing the peace and comfort of your own home to somewhere which may be noisy and depressing.

Early in the week, start making a check list of all the items of kit you want to take with you. Take a bit too much, rather than too little, and keep adding to the list as you think of things while on a training run, washing up, or travelling home from work. Then, before you leave, go religiously through the list as you pack your bags. It won't be much fun to arrive at the race and realize that your shoes are still under the kitchen table.

In addition to the usual items of kit, you should include Vaseline, an emergency plastic bag for storing your tracksuit if necessary, spare shoelaces (they always break at the wrong moment), a tin of assorted plasters (for use before or after the race), plus any other medical items you may feel necessary, wads of toilet paper (it frequently runs out in the changing rooms, and some tucked into your shorts during the race may prove a blessing too), and your favourite refreshments for after the race.

If you are running abroad, remember that in Europe, for example, it is often impossible to get cereal for breakfast. So take your own, together with any other accustomed items of pre-race food you feel you need. Don't rely on being able to get them at the race venue. I remember Joyce Smith sitting in the hotel on the morning of the 1979 Avon International Women's Marathon in West Germany, making up sandwiches of brown bread and honey which she had brought specially from England, while other runners watched, goggle-eyed. But it was ideal for her, psychologically and nutritionally, and she won the race in a Commonwealth record of 2 hours 36 minutes 27 seconds.

If you are going to tape your toes as a precaution against blistering, the night before is often a good opportunity. Wind short overlapping lengths of half-inch sticking plaster around each toe individually, firmly, but not cutting off the circulation! Overnight it will set and mould to your toes like an extra layer of skin.

This is a particularly therapeutic occupation. For not only are you concentrating your mind on the race, and doing something of practical value in preparation for it, but you are also substituting a kind of related physical activity. It is often difficult to concentrate fully on anything other than those 26 miles getting nearer and nearer.

The Day of the Race

On race day, aim to arrive at the changing rooms some 90 minutes before the start unless there is a special reason for arriving earlier (at the Duchy of Cornwall Marathon, for example, competitors are taken to the start at Land's End in buses, then run the 26 miles back to Redruth). But assuming the race will start near by, that should be long enough to attend to the necessary.

Collect your number from the officials' table, and if you have personal drinks remember to mark your race number (which you may not know until you arrive at the venue) on your bottles before handing them in.

You may find yourself visiting the toilets several times as nerves increase, but take every opportunity to clear bowels and bladder 'ready for action'. Re-read the instructions sent to runners, which may explain all you need to know about the race. Surprisingly, not everyone does.

Decide what you are going to wear in the race itself, based on how hot/cold/wet/windy it appears to be, and pin the numbers to whatever will be your top layer in the race. If it is hot, stay in a cool place for as long as possible, not in the sun, and sit or lie down for part of the time, trying to relax as much as you can.

Study a course map, because even if you are not going to be in the lead, it will be a great help to know roughly where you are in relation to the finish at any point. The better-organized races will have regular mile markers, and time checks.

Are there any steep hills on the course? If you haven't run it before, ask someone who has, or an official. Check the programme to see if it includes a course description.

Leaving a tracksuit during the race can be a problem, and not simply for reasons of security. If you are accompanied by someone to the race, of course, they can look after it. This is probably the most acceptable plan, as long as they know you will need it as soon as you finish and they don't go charging off round the course with it, or lock it in the boot of their car and disappear with the key.

At races where the start and finish are at different points, the organizers usually provide a numbered plastic bag in which you can put your gear, and they will take it to the finish, where you reclaim the bag by showing your race number.

But one of the disadvantages of a race as big as the New York City Marathon, where so many thousands of athletes have to gather at the start early in the morning, is that tracksuits which have to be taken to the finish must be handed in at least 30 minutes before the 10.30 a.m. start. This means that for half an hour or more, the runners could otherwise be stripped off waiting to run, and in cold, windy conditions like the 1980 race, that is no joke. So in such circumstances, the well-prepared runner will take along an old sweater and trousers to keep over his running gear until a few minutes from the start. Then, he discards the old clothes forever (at New York, special containers are provided by the organizers, and any useable clothing is washed and passed on to charity). At the finish he simply picks up his tracksuit, as at any other race.

Again, reuniting an exhausted runner with his tracksuit becomes a bigger problem as marathons expand. With thousands of runners, can a friend or relative easily find the specific body needed to fit the tracksuit they hold anyway? In such cases, the numbered bag system would seem ideal, as long as there is someone to organize the bags numerically at the reclaim area during the race. But I have been at marathons where the mass search for bags among thousands stacked indiscriminately on a huge floor has been reminiscent of the January sales rush, and is totally impractical.

Usually the best plan is to have some kind of 'fail-safe' system, involving a second, or even third, set of clothing stored at a guaranteed point if your original kit goes temporarily missing for whatever reason. At the end of a marathon, particularly on a bad day, you simply cannot take a chance on having to wander around shivering in a search for your tracksuit.

After the Race

You will not need advice on the very first thing you want to do when you cross the finishing line. Between them, your mind and body will have been telling you for some miles that you want to (a) take these wretched shoes off; (b) lie down on some cool grass; (c) get another drink; (d) be sick; or (e) jump up and down like a dervish in celebration at having completed the course.

The initial reactions are, most popularly, 'It's over!' closely followed by 'Never again!' – although the desire will probably return sooner rather than later.

But first you want to get this one out of the way. After your initial reaction – whether it is (a) to (e), or something quite different – check your feet for any blisters or toenail damage which might require first-aid treatment, and seek out the St John Ambulance if necessary.

If you get any attacks of cramp, they can be relieved by stretching the affected muscle fully; persistent cramp may need massage. Those frequently affected could try taking salt tablets before and after the race.

Unfortunately, it is rarely possible to have a warm bath at the finish of a marathon, but showers, even lukewarm, can still be very refreshing.

You will almost certainly want to drink more liquid at the finish, and there is usually another refreshment table near by. You may not want to eat anything solid for some hours afterwards, as your appetite diminishes and your thirst increases during the race. But some hours later your stomach will certainly tell you that it is ready for a good meal.

Try to walk round for a while after you have first recovered, to keep the circulation moving, which in turn may help to shift the fatigue debris from your muscles and lead to less stiffness next day.

The official times from the race will normally be posted up near the dressing room as soon as they are available, so don't worry the timekeepers unnecessarily by peering over their shoulders while they are still trying to record other runners home. You may distract them, and someone may be missed altogether. Usually full result sheets are sent out in the week or two after the race, together with any time certificates to which you may be entitled.

Before you leave for home, make sure you have all your belongings (a vast amount of kit is often left behind by mistake), collect any of your personal drink bottles which may have been picked up and returned. But don't create a fuss if they go missing; there is nothing in the rules about the organizers being obliged to return them to you, and they are not that expensive anyway.

Offering a very brief word of thanks to any of the race officials you may come across after the race, whether it's the linch-pin organizer of the whole race or a marker in a plastic orange waistcoat, will never go amiss. Even raising your hand in acknowledgement to a marker during the race will show him that you at least appreciate him giving up four hours of Grandstand to endure wind and rain on this exposed, isolated corner. He may even have rather been doing what you're doing.

On the day after the race, and the day after that, you will almost certainly be feeling some degree of leg stiffness, even to the extent of finding it easier to walk up and down the stairs backwards, to relieve pain in the thighs and hamstrings. But jogging even half a mile or a mile very gently each day, followed by a hot bath, will help ease the stiffness. It may take as long as a fortnight before you are back in full training again, but most people find that within that time they are already planning their next marathon.

It is best to wait at least three months before tackling another, to ensure you have recovered fully and can start building up afresh for the next, rather than simply repairing the damage from the last one. The first marathon is always a question of 'Can I get round?'; after that, it is a question of 'How can I get round faster?'

The 'Wall' and the Carbohydrate Loading Diet

The simple question of 'How can I run faster?' when posed by some of the world's leading international marathon runners is not that simple any more. But in the past decade or so it has led to the widespread adoption of (and in some cases disenchantment with) various 'carbohydrate loading' techniques, which have helped some runners achieve quicker times, others to perform well below their best, and generally caused a great deal of controversy in the marathon world.

The relatively recent introduction of such techniques, whose principle is to manipulate the diet into providing additional energy fuel, has meant that even physiologists, let alone the runners themselves, are still somewhat divided on the relative merits and drawbacks of the system. No one knows, either, whether there are any long-term effects of what is actually a method of deliberately tampering with the body's chemistry.

The background is this. Marathon runners have long recognized that there comes a point in the later stages of the race, usually between 18–23 miles, when running suddenly becomes very much harder. From running quite comfortably they are suddenly, without warning, dragged down to a much slower pace, despite increased effort. The change is accompanied by weak legs, acute muscle discomfort and fatigue, together with doubts about even finishing. Remember Bernie Ford's description (page 83) of his first marathon experience? 'I never knew that any race could be transformed so quickly. One minute it was unbelievably easy, the next unbelievably difficult.'

That sensation in the race is commonly known as 'hitting the Wall', because that is very much what it feels like. Every race in athletics has its equivalent crucial moment. A 400 metres runner hits it around 300 metres, and it has been said, graphically and accurately, that the winner of a 400 metres race is not the athlete running the fastest, but the one who slows down the least. That description could apply equally well to the marathon.

For what has happened is that after approximately 20 miles of hard running, the muscles have used up all their chief energy-providing source, glycogen (which is stored carbohydrate, in the form of sugar), and a chain reaction sets in as new stocks of fuel are urgently sought by the muscles.

The body switches to a readily available, but less efficient, alternative: fat. The fitter and more experienced in long runs you are, then the quicker and more easily this transition takes place. No one, claim physiologists, can avoid hitting the Wall at some stage, using up all of their glycogen, if they have run hard for the full 26 miles. But some hit it harder than others.

The leading runners sometimes tend not to notice. Some even claim they have never hit the Wall. What they mean is that they have not *noticed* the effects of doing so, probably because they were concentrating so hard on the race itself. But they will still have had to work that much harder in the closing miles just to maintain an even pace, while those who hit the Wall hardest may slow by anything up to 3 minutes a mile or more.

So that was the problem which faced the world's fastest runners at the end of the sixties, when they were already doing a tremendous volume of training mileage, which could scarcely be increased significantly without openly inviting leg muscle or bone injury from overuse.

The whole field of 'carbohydrate loading' diets was first opened up by Swedish physiologists who were experimenting at that time with ways of increasing the muscle glycogen content in long-distance cyclists. They developed a method of deliberately depleting the glycogen some time before competition, and then boosting the replacement stores by dietary adjustment.

The first link with marathon running came through Ron Hill, who was told of the experiments by an international teammate.

Appreciating its value in possibly delaying the moment in a marathon race at which the runner hits the Wall, Hill tried out the technique for the first time in the 1969 AAA championship race in Manchester, and beat Australia's Derek Clayton by 2 minutes, moving into the lead at 15 miles, and winning in 2:13.42 (then the second fastest-ever time by a British runner).

Two months later he tried it again in the European Championships race in Athens. Although by the 19 miles mark he was in third place, feeling tired, and had already settled for the bronze medal, in the last 7 miles he found himself sweeping through with apparent ease into first place. He turned a deficit of 1½ minutes on the leader into a winning margin of 45 seconds by the finishing line, to record the first of a series of major international marathon victories.

The Techniques:

The fullest and most severe version of the carbohydrate loading diet technique is divided into three distinct sections, as follows:

1. Seven days before your race (say the Sunday before a Saturday marathon) you take a very long run, perhaps 20 miles or more, to deliberately deplete the glycogen currently in your muscles. You 'run to the Wall', in fact. (Some physiologists suggest a shorter distance, but followed by a series of hard interval runs over, say, 400 metres, will also result in sufficient depletion.)
2. After that session, and for the next three days, you take very few carbohydrates in your diet, but live on a mainly high protein and fat diet, while continuing to train very lightly.
3. From Wednesday lunchtime you switch to a high percentage carbohydrate diet (bread, cereals, cake, doughnuts, chocolate etc.), while still taking in fats, proteins, vitamins and minerals, and still training lightly.

The theory behind this is based on the Swedish experiment which showed that by intentionally using up all the glycogen first (a process known as the 'bleed-out'), followed by a near abstinence from carbohydrates for three days, you can stimulate the body into producing extra glycogen-storing enzymes, and these will eventually allow the muscles to store an even greater amount of glycogen than they could before.

Then, when the diet is switched back to its high carbohydrate level from lunchtime on Wednesday, the amount of stored glycogen can reach almost double the normal level.

But, like everything in this world, it is not quite as simple as that. Otherwise it would undoubtedly be in wider use than it is. But for a start the athlete using the most severe form of the system has to endure three days of possible depression, while feeling jaded, tired, irritable, possibly sleeping badly, and being particularly prone to catching any flu or cold germs which may be in the vicinity, as the body is so low in its resistance at that time. From Wednesday, the intake of cakes and Mars bars can be very enjoyable, but because training all week is kept to a very light level, partly to preserve the maximum of glycogen for Saturday, but partly too because the runner may not be feeling very energetic for much of the time, there is often a weight increase. A higher liquid intake is necessary too, because stored glycogen needs a considerable amount of water (3–4 lbs of it may be stored per lb of glycogen) and if that water is not provided by the diet, the body will take it from elsewhere, leading to possible dehydration.

So you go to the starting line, not having run particularly well, or far, for nearly a week, feeling somewhat lethargic and bloated, and knowing that you are several pounds heavier than usual. It needs a great deal of confidence in those circumstances to feel that you are still going to run well.

Some athletes have survived the diet regularly with honour; others now feel that an illness suffered just before a major international race was due entirely to the 'early week blues'; and still others point out that the difference between their best time in a marathon using the diet, and their best time without it, are just a few seconds apart.

In fact, no two athletes probably react in exactly the same way. And there is medical opinion that the diet should not be used more than two or three times a year, because any possible long-term effects which this repeated 'fooling' of your body may cause are unknown, and because of the fact that in any case the body soon realizes its chemistry is being manipulated, and adapts accordingly. Then the method is not so effective. In any case, it should never be tried by anyone suffering from a condition like diabetes.

Ron Hill, with 20 years of international marathoning behind him, has now modified his own views on the diet through his varied experiments, trying different combinations of depletion and high and low carbohydrate diets. For a start, he says, he has never been an advocate of the initial 20 miles 'bleed-out' run, because 'to me it seems crazy to run 20 miles at any pace only a week before a marathon'. He feels that the glycogen can be depleted on less, and he brings about depletion by running twice each day (his normal routine) with hard runs on the second session of the first and second days of the week; then he runs easily on the third.

During these first three days, on the low carbohydrate phase, he still eats eggs, cheese, bacon, ham, cooked meats (boiled ham or tongue), butter, fish, other meats (chicken, steak, chops) together with green salads, tomatoes and other vegetables, such as carrots, turnips, cabbage, cauliflower, peas and beans (but no potatoes). He avoids the obvious sweet and starchy foods, but permits himself four Ryvita biscuits (instead of bread), an apple, an orange and a yoghurt each day.

He emphasizes that carbohydrates should not be totally eliminated from the diet during the first phase, because some are needed just to support the vital life processes. In his early days with the diet, though, he went beyond this.

'After the initial successes, the more I refined the diet, up to the 1972 Munich Olympics, the worse it became. I simply didn't understand what was happening, or the fact that if you cut out carbohydrates completely during the early part of the week before the race, still train hard and deplete your glycogen level, but go past that point, then you're actually harming yourself.'

When he switches back to carbohydrates on the Wednesday now, he satisfies the immediate craving for sweet foods, but takes care not to overstuff himself on the next two days because he has experienced indigestion problems, and in any case feels that his normal diet is sufficiently high in carbohydrates to 'load' the muscles when combined with his lighter pre-race training programme. His own experiences have indicated that, while it is not for everybody, the diet has certainly worked for him in the past, and he notices a quicker recovery rate after the race than when he doesn't use it.

A warning on the effects of overloading comes from Dr Gabe Mirkin, an American running nutrition expert, who points out that once the enzymes in the muscle tissue are 'overprimed' to receive extra glycogen stores, they will store all that is offered to them: 'And once glycogen is stored, it cannot get out. You have to burn it off, otherwise it will keep accumulating until the muscle tissue bursts. Runners who have loaded for more than three days, or whose muscles fill to capacity in only two days, have done themselves considerable damage on the diet.'

Because of its possibly negative psychological effects in the early part of the week, more and more runners are turning instead to an abbreviated version of the diet, where a depletion run of around 12 miles is done four days before the race. No carbohydrates are eaten for the rest of that day, but the athlete switches *next* day to the high carbohydrate intake, and can still achieve a relatively high proportion of the loading effect.

Other runners are simply content to eat more carbohydrates in their normal diet in the last three days before a marathon (spaghetti, pizza and pasta are popular eve-of-marathon dishes) without depleting at all. The night before the race is the last to eat heavily; on the morning of the race, light foods like cereal, toast or scrambled eggs should suffice, so that the stomach is not still trying to digest heavy food when the race starts.

The term 'placebo' has even been used of the full carbohydrate loading system by the more cynical. But if you can survive the traumatic period between the bleed-out stage and getting to the 20-mile point in the race itself, then it may suddenly become a big mental, as much as physical, boost.

Another simpler, and more recently proposed, recipe for delaying the arrival of the Wall is the good old cup of coffee. The noted US physiologist David Costill has recommended two cups of black coffee, drunk about an hour before the start, as possibly helping the athlete to run faster. The caffeine in it apparently allows the burning of a greater amount of the free-floating fats in the blood system for energy earlier in the race, and thus helping to postpone the eventual exhaustion of available glycogen.

'I play down the caffeine now, because it's a drug,' says Costill, 'and I don't want anyone to feel they have to do the equivalent of taking a pill in order to turn in a good performance. But it does seem to facilitate fat metabolism, and that in turn delays glycogen depletion.'

What must never be forgotten, though, is that the whole idea of the carbohydrate loading diet was originally taken up by international runners *who had reached the virtual limit of their possible training load*. What it can never, ever do is to replace the hundreds and hundreds of training miles which you have to put into your marathon preparation first. It is no good spending time, effort and discomfort arranging in advance for your triumphant blast through the infamous Wall at 22 miles if you have to drop out exhausted after only 8 miles through lack of fitness. And in any case such diets are definitely not recommended for first time marathoners.

As Bill Adcocks says, sometimes we may put too much emphasis on diet, shoes, and so on. Of course they have to be right too, and you won't get far if you don't normally eat a reasonable, balanced diet, or if your shoes are too tight. But above all, even if you have the right diet and the right shoes, you will still not get anywhere if you haven't made your main priority training sufficiently hard in the first place.

7

Injuries (and other pains)

Fairly early on in life, from the time you first try to run, you find that this peculiar activity, if continued beyond an initial burst, often brings with it, in addition to fatigue and breathlessness, other ailments. And as you pursue running to a greater and greater degree, so the ailments become more complex, painful and restricting. They range in severity from 'stitch' to a cracked limb, which can all be brought on by the simple process of putting one foot in front of the other thousands and thousands of times.

The first running ailment we ever came across may have been at the school sports, or even in the playground, where most of us have protested, 'Hang on a minute, I've got a stitch.'

The onset of **stitch**, generally recognized as a sharp pain in the side, or even the shoulder, is usually attributed in runners to a spasm of the diaphragm. There have been many theories about cause and cure, and some causes are obvious. Running too soon after a heavy meal, for instance, can cause stitch. But even Basil Heatley, Britain's silver medallist in the 1964 Olympic marathon, suffered stitch in that race, and he certainly didn't have a big meal beforehand.

Emptying the bladder immediately before running causes stitch in some runners; *not* doing so causes it in others. There is no single apparent cause. And the only reasonable form of treatment once it hits you seems to be to ease off your running pace until it passes, which is extremely frustrating to say the least, but the pain often inhibits your normal breathing too.

My own preferred method of getting rid of it, reached merely through personal trial and error, is to run 'tall', lifting the body from the waist, and trying to stretch out any poor form in running style which may be caused through a slight loll to one side or the other. It usually works for me, but I can't guarantee what it will do for you.

Another problem for runners of all standards are common or garden **blisters**. They are caused by the skin rubbing against an unyielding surface or edge inside the running shoe. A seam, or even a crease or darn in a sock, can cause them too. Sometimes they are quite unpredictable in their occurrence, although usually with hindsight it is relatively easy to find the cause once the damage is done.

The softer skin of the novice is more susceptible than that of the experienced runner, but in a marathon no one is ever totally immune from the potential blistering effects of a shoe on the feet during 26 miles of hard running. The feet swell during exercise, for example, pushing the skin surface right against irritating seams or surfaces which seemed quite comfortable beforehand.

Clear blisters, where the outer layer of skin (epidermis) separates from the inner layer (dermis), and a watery blood compound called serum is sent to 'pad' the area of friction, are quite simple to treat. A sterilized needle is used to puncture the outer surface, which is a painless operation, and the fluid is squeezed out and mopped up with cotton wool. The treatment may need to be repeated two or three times to clear all of the fluid. Then the area is cleaned with disinfectant, covered with Elastoplast or similar protection, and in many cases the two skin layers may reattach within days. Where the outer surface is broken, the skin will eventually dry up and drop off, to be replaced from beneath.

Sometimes, though, the blister will be seen to be full of reddish-brown blood, and in these cases it should not be broken because of the risk of infection getting into the blood stream. You should clean, pad and cover the area, and try to avoid making the blister worse by again wearing the same shoes which caused it until it has completely cleared.

Prevention is better than cure when possible. Before a long race, sticking plaster applied carefully to areas prone to blistering (the tops of the toes, and around the ankles, for instance) can help to prevent, or at least delay, blistering. Vaseline over the toes can reduce friction, and an alternative is talcum powder sprinkled into the shoes and socks, which helps to absorb moisture. A few extra minutes spent on such precautions before a marathon can even make the difference between finishing and not finishing.

Black toenails are another occupational hazard of long-distance running, and are caused by shoes which do not fit properly, so that the toe is jammed hard against the roof of the shoe on every step. The toe starts to bleed under the nail, and the blood causes a painful build-up of pressure.

Although the nail may then die, to be slowly replaced by a new growth some weeks later, it is meanwhile fairly tender. One recommended method of alleviating the pain is to straighten out a paper clip, heat one end strongly in a flame, and then put the point of the clip on the centre of the nail, which has a gelatin-like consistency, and will melt. Make a small hole in the nail with this, then apply downward pressure to both sides of the nail and the fluid will shoot through the hole created by the hot paper clip. Mop up, clean the area with antiseptic, and cover it with plaster. The nail may remain tender for some days afterwards, and you should avoid running in the shoes which caused the problem.

To prevent it happening again, make two small slits (or even a hole) in the shoe over the point at which the nail was rubbing in the first place to eliminate the pressure. If the shoes are too narrow anyway, consider replacing them, because the chances are that another nail will be similarly affected next time.

Cramp is a sudden and sustained spasm of a muscle, and can also be very painful, not to mention unexpected. Medical experts say that it has not yet been fully explained, but an imbalance of electrolyte and fluid (often caused by excessive sweating) is certainly one cause. It can affect the legs during the closing stages of a marathon, and the immediate treatment is to stretch the affected muscle to halt the spasm, stop or walk, and gently massage the area before gingerly starting to jog again.

The Olympic runner Tony Simmons has been particularly prone to cramp in marathons, and in the last mile of the 1978 Sandbach Marathon was almost forced out of the race while well in the lead when a spectator waved to a TV camera, knocking into Simmons and causing both of his legs to seize up temporarily. Fortunately, he got going again and won the race.

The prolonged, unchanging use of a certain muscle group can also increase the likelihood of cramp, and ironically a marathon course with one or two hills in the latter stages, where a slightly different running action is used to tackle the incline, may be less likely to cause cramp than a totally flat, unremitting course with no such contrasts.

Even after the race or a long training session has been survived unscathed, a slight overstretch in bed at night has awakened many a runner from a pleasant dream with a searing leg cramp, causing him to roll around the floor in search of a suitable position for relief (much to the surprise of their spouse). Occasionally, trying to relieve one leg sets off a cramp in the other, and so on. It is not so funny at the time for the affected runner, but it can be quite a spectacle for bystanders.

For the beginner, muscle groups used in unfamiliar style to excess are also liable to cramp. As an example, I was team-managing a group of British runners at the Essonne Marathon in 1980, where the organizers lent me a bicycle to enable me to follow the race more closely. I hadn't ridden a bike for years, and I had to pedal it quite fast to cut across sections of the course, especially after getting lost on unfamiliar roads.

That night the reception for the competitors was rudely interrupted by me jumping up from our table with sudden cramp spasms in the hamstring and quadriceps from the cycle riding. Explanatory word went round to the other tables: the runners are all okay, but the team manager has got cramp.

Injuries

Even the fittest sportsman in the world walks a very narrow tightrope between being a finely tuned, magnificent physical specimen, and a limping wreck. And, whatever your standard, as a long distance runner you will not be able to escape without, at the very minimum, the odd ache and pain, brought about simply by the constant repetition of the running action on hard, unremitting surfaces like roads.

'Most marathon runners will have injury problems, but these are of a limited variety and unspectacular from a medical point of view,' says Dr Ian Adams, Medical Adviser to the British Marathon Runners Club, sounding almost disappointed. 'Stopping running will cure these injuries, which are generally caused by minor abnormalities which are of no significance in the general population, so do not be surprised if the doctor does not welcome you with open arms, and advises rest.

'The great majority of injuries will occur through breaking simple rules of training. Just as many of us, in spite of prodigious training, could not be top-class sprinters, there are others with structural faults which will never withstand 100 miles per week for month after month. We are all different heights and weights, we all have different shaped knees and feet, some made for high mileage whilst others are made for limited mileage. There are injuries which can be directly treated, there are others which can be indirectly treated, and there are some which are untreatable in the context of running 100 miles per week.'

A runner covering even 20 to 30 miles a week in training will still be taking something like 2,000,000 strides in a year, and it only needs a slight imbalance, possibly caused by a worn-down shoe or an irritating blister, to throw the whole complex machine out of sync. If you realize that it is not just your bodyweight, but a significantly increased force (around 500 lbs for a 10-stone man) which is being absorbed through your legs on every stride, then the frequency of injury among distance runners is less surprising.

Most injuries in marathon runners occur in the lower leg and foot, and apart from an unlucky accident, like putting your foot down a hole or treading on a stone, nearly all are caused by the vast number of times the same running action is repeated. This type of injury is called an *overuse* injury.

Such injuries are particularly frustrating because you know that in order to improve as a marathon runner you have to run as much as possible, and yet when you have an overuse injury you have to stop, or at least curtail, your running for an initially unspecified period.

Knowing exactly how long you will have to rest is one of those problems to which there is no definite answer. Experienced runners use a combination of the reduced pain messages being sent from the injury, plus intuition, to decide when to return to the fray. Others, less wisely, adopt the same combination, but subtract a week, and are usually sidelined again three days later.

A few muscle injuries can be 'run through', but the first question with any running injury should always be 'What caused it?' If you are able to run pain-free for months, and then suddenly you have a leg injury, there must be a reason. Have you turned an ankle over? Are your shoes worn down at the heel, causing you to run awkwardly and also over-stretching the Achilles tendons? Have you increased the training load significantly in a short space of time? Have you suddenly switched to a different training surface? Or different shoes? Are you now repeatedly running uphill? Do you have some natural imbalance (check to see whether one shoe is worn down more than the other) which could be causing the problem? Do you often run on the camber of a road, so that one leg action is slightly restricted?

If you can pinpoint this type of injury-cause – some change in your routine at about the time the injury was first noticed – then you have won half the battle. Removing, or adjusting, the cause should help to clear up the injury.

But if you do carry on running with an injured foot or leg, you have to be careful to avoid 'favouring' it subconsciously. For example, if you have a knee pain and you try to continue activity, the chances are that, without realizing it, you will soon be taking additional force on the ankle of the opposite leg in an effort to reduce the pain shooting through your knee on every stride. Then that ankle will start to ache.

There is no guaranteed method of preventing injuries, but simple mobility exercises before a training run will help to cut down the chance of injury among distance runners, who are notorious in the athletics world for usually being about as supple as a plank of teak.

Only a small percentage of distance runners, I would guess, actually do mobility exercises at all, with the rest reasoning that the 10 minutes or so they would spend could be better used by putting in another 1–1½ miles of running. Perhaps, but then add up all the miles which could be missed through avoidable injury!

Exercise sessions vary. Track runners may spend anything up to an hour going through a programme of graduated exercises, designed to hyper-extend each set of muscles and joints they will shortly be using for flat-out speed work. By slowly and deliberately stretching them, a safety-margin is being introduced before the action starts. For if the muscles only ever reach their greatest extension during high speed running, then the chance of injury is that much greater.

The same theory, on a smaller scale, should apply to distance runners, particularly before training in the morning, when the body is stiff, and when the majority of injuries begin. Simple stretching exercises for the Achilles tendons, hamstrings, quadriceps, groin, knees and ankles can help prepare the legs for the period of exercise ahead. Boring? Possibly, but less so than not being able to run at all because of injury.

The most common leg injuries among long distance runners are those affecting the Achilles tendon, knee and shin.

The **Achilles tendon**, which attaches the calf muscle to the heel bone, may be the site of a lot of pain (tendinitis) for beginner and experienced runner alike. In its mildest form, which can include some swelling and tenderness to the touch, it may be brought on simply by the new runner overdoing it with too much running in the early stages, or by trying to run on the toes. The natural distance running action is to land on the heel, and then roll forward on to the ball of the foot, and push off with the toes.

In more experienced runners, worn down heels on running shoes, which cause the tendon to be stretched beyond its normal extension on every stride, are a frequent cause of tendon pain, while a switch to a lot of uphill running, or to shoes with little heel support (particularly spiked shoes among track runners) are also potential causes.

Again, correcting the problem will usually also cure the injury, although putting some temporary sponge heel pads in the shoes, and avoiding oversoft surfaces, like mud or sand, may help. Running on firm cinder paths or flat grassland is best during recovery.

You should also ensure that the heels of your everyday shoes are not so high as to cause too great a contrast in range of tendon movement when you switch to running shoes in the evening. In the more severe cases of tendinitis, immobilization, or even surgery, may be necessary.

Runner's knee, sometimes called (but not all that often!) *chondromalacia patellae*, is believed to be caused by a softening of the cartilage of the undersurface of the kneecap (patella), which normally moves over the end of the femur, or thigh bone. This softening may be caused by excessive rotation of the knee as the foot hits the ground, possibly due to the athlete being slightly knock-kneed, bow-legged, or having a foot imbalance.

Arch supports in the shoes to correct the imbalance have worked with success in the past after one US running doctor had accidentally found his own problem with Runner's Knee had vanished temporarily when he ran on a road camber. Exercises to strengthen the quadriceps are also recommended by some doctors.

The knee is the shock absorber of the body, the Clapham Junction of the leg, with bones, muscles, tendons and ligaments being anchored at this joint. Torn cartilage and strained ligaments are other causes of knee pain, and, if it is persistent, medical help should be sought.

Shin soreness consists of a sharp pain and tightness on the outside of the shin. The problem arises because the anterior tibial (shin) muscles, which also support the arch mechanism of the foot, have little room to expand, as they do during sustained exercise. The subsequent build-up of pressure within the restraining sheath restricts blood circulation.

A high training mileage, running shoe soles which do not flex sufficiently (so that a high degree of shock is absorbed in the shin), and imbalance of strength between shin and calf muscles, are all possible causes. Treatment can involve a switch to softer training surfaces, and application of ice packs on the affected shins two or three times a day for 5 to 10 minutes at a time. Rotating several different pairs of training shoes, to allow for a slightly different foot balance each time, may also help, but wearing anything which grips tightly around the lower leg (like knee socks) should be avoided. Even then, rest may eventually prove to be the only answer.

Severe shin soreness should be treated with suspicion for a possible stress fracture, which is a very common injury among runners who put in a high training load on hard surfaces. The **stress fracture** usually occurs in the tibia or fibula of the lower leg, or in the metatarsals of the foot.

The symptoms in the leg are similar to shin soreness, with sometimes local swelling and tenderness just above the ankle, where the constant stresses across the long bone may have produced a tiny crack which will not always show up on X-ray. As treatment, rest from running will normally allow the bone to heal completely in around four to six weeks, but runners hate being inactive for that length of time if it is at all avoidable.

So other forms of exercises, like swimming and cycling, can, if performed with sufficient gusto, enable the cardiovascular system to at least retain some condition without hurting the leg, although such activities can never actually replace running. Some easy jogging on grass is often possible, even in the early days of healing too, but such activity should be treated with great caution, and any adverse signs from the leg (or foot) should be noted and acted upon immediately.

Even after healing, too much road work should be avoided, and to start back on the road too soon (or even to ignore the injury altogether) could result in the need for complete immobilization in a plaster cast.

In such circumstances, impatience is probably the distance runner's worst enemy. Every day of inactivity is multiplied in the mind by X minutes or Y miles of running. But the body takes a fair old battering in the course of marathon training: leg-jarring pounding, coupled with great fatigue, which almost inevitably, by its very nature, will result in some kind of physical breakdown sooner or later.

The runner is always searching for the magic formula which will allow him to take one more pace further forward than before, but without injury. Then one more, and one more, until – Twang-Krukkk!

When you reach the stage of Twang-Krukkk! your main objective suddenly switches from being able to run faster to simply being able to run again. It is always a frustrating time, when most runners suffer from training withdrawal symptoms and get irritable, introspective and unsociable. Unless it is to talk about their injury, of course. 'Good evening, your Majesty. Did you hear about my cracked metatarsal? Just hold my shoe a minute, and I'll show you. . . .'

8

Which Marathon?

Having trained hard, bought the right shoes, eaten the correct food, and guarded meticulously against blisters, chafing and stitch, you may at this stage be short of only one vital ingredient – a marathon in which to run. So how do you discover which marathons are taking place, when, where, and how do you enter them?

The most effective way for even the very experienced runner is by simply watching the Coming Events columns and advertisements for races at home and abroad in the specialist magazines, which include:

Athletics Weekly
344 High St
Rochester
Kent ME1 1DT

Athlete's World (monthly)
Marathon Runner (monthly)
Peterson House
Northbank
Berryhill Industrial Estate
Droitwich
Worcs. WR9 9BL

Running Magazine (monthly)
57–61 Mortimer St
London W1

Running Review
2 Tower St
Hyde
Cheshire

Most (although not all) of the races will state in their advertisements that the event will be held 'Under Amateur Athletic Association and Women's Amateur Athletic Association Laws'. For athletics is still almost entirely an amateur sport, and if any of the thousands of amateur club runners in this country were to knowingly compete in a race which was not held under the recognized amateur laws, then he or she would theoretically become ineligible for further competition, regardless of whether a prize had been won or not.

The amateur code has long been a bone of contention and controversy in athletics, and never was the upholding of these rules put to such a widespread test as it is now. Thousands of runners who know or care little for the finer points of the amateur rules, which have been abandoned in other sports, are pouring into the marathon world, and officials realistically have little chance of closely controlling the situation with so many people involved. If there were simply no amateur definition, it would make it a lot less complicated. But for the time being the rules exist, and it is as well to know about them.

As part of its own adaptation to the situation, the AAA changed its ruling with regard to 'unattached' runners in the summer of 1981. Previously it was not possible to compete as 'unattached' (i.e. not a member of an affiliated club) for longer than twelve months. At the end of that time, an unattached runner had to join a recognized club. Now that is no longer the case but, in certain events, such as the London Marathon, the unattached entrant will have to pay an extra premium on their entry free so that the day-to-day administrators of the sport will still receive some benefit, which it misses if the runner does not join an athletics club.

For some of the new wave of runners may have little or no particular interest in formal track and field athletics as such, and for them new-style groups like the London Road Runners Club (see page 147) may be the best answer as to which club to join. It is a club duly affiliated to the AAA, but confining its own activities strictly to road running for all abilities. There are, of course, hundreds of equally suitable established athletics clubs all round the country too.

The whereabouts of your nearest club, if inquiries at the local sports centre or recreation department fail to unearth one, may be discovered by writing to the honorary secretary of the relevant regional association:

Southern Counties AAA
Francis House
Francis St
London SW1
(01-828-8640)

Welsh Women's AAA
19 Coed Bach
Highlight Estate
Barry

Midland Counties AAA
Devonshire House
High St
Deritend
Birmingham B12 0LP
(021-773-1631)

Scottish AAA
16 Royal Crescent
Glasgow G3 7SL
(041-332-5144)

Northern Counties AA
Studio 44
Bluecoat Chambers
School Lane
Liverpool L1 3BX
(051-708-9363)

Scottish Women's AAA
16 Royal Crescent
Glasgow G3 7SL
(041-332-9304)

Women's AAA
Francis House
Francis St
London SW1
(01-828-4731)

N. Ireland AAA
20 Kernan Park
Portadown
Co Armagh, NI

Welsh AAA
'Winterbourne'
Greenway Close
Llandough
Penarth
South Glamorgan
CF6 1LZ

N. Ireland Women's AAA
8 Broadway Avenue
Ballymena, NI

Events organized under the Laws of the AAA, the Women's AAA, and equivalent bodies, also impose certain age-restrictions on participants in long distance running. Until the summer of 1981 the limits laid down by the AAA were clearly set out in their own Handbook, but the relatively sudden decision of the Association then to reduce the minimum age for running a marathon from twenty to eighteen meant that some of the previous limits (under which an eighteen-year-old male runner had only been able to race 25 km, or 15½ miles) were made redundant. Eventually a new limit was set for other ages too. A sixteen-year-old may now run up to 15 km (9½ miles), while a seventeen-year-old may run up to 25 km (15½ miles), an eighteen-year-old up to 50 km (31 miles), and for distances above 50 km the runners must be over twenty. Ages are reckoned on day of competition.

The Women's AAA also lowered its age groups to allow eighteen-year-old girls to run the full marathon from 1981, and amended its other limits as follows:

Age at 31 Aug./1 Sep. prior to race	*Race distance must not exceed*
15	10 km (6¼ miles)
16	15 km (9½ miles)
17	25 km (15½ miles)
18 (on day of race)	No limit

There are some running events where these Laws, and therefore the age-restrictions, do not apply. If an event which is not held under the recognized amateur laws, but is advertised merely as a 'run' rather than a race (i.e. there are no official winners, results or prizes), then such an event may well be interpreted as allowing participation without endangering amateur status.

The popular Masters and Maidens Marathon in Surrey (see page 138) probably comes into this category. It is a *timed run* rather than a race, and afterwards it lists *fastest times* rather than a finishing order or result. There are no prize winners, and although we may only be playing with words here, it is generally accepted now as a genuine 'fun run' event.

But other unsanctioned events, which offer prizes in cash or kind, are out of bounds to any runner wishing to retain amateur status for future competition under AAA Laws. Remember that the London Marathon, for just one example, is held under AAA Laws, and open only to those eligible to compete under those laws.

The grey area of overlap is getting greyer all the time, but if you are in doubt about the status of any event in which you intend to participate, check with your area athletics association.

There are now many fund-raising charity runs around the country with organizers and participants alike blissfully unaware of any rules of amateur athletics which they may be contravening. In most cases, it doesn't matter, nor should it, as the two worlds may stay apart. But if you try to participate in every running event which comes along, sooner or later you may run into the rule book.

The pages which follow list a cross-section of established marathons in the UK and abroad, as a guide to some of those which are available. But a word of caution. Some of these races impose time or numerical limits on entry, which may change; others, in the current running boom, may decide to introduce them in the near future.

Courses, mostly on public roads, are always subject to alteration from time to time, either through the choice of the organizers, the advice of the police, or the necessity of gas, electricity and water companies to simultaneously start digging up the stretch of road which previously constituted the 7th mile.

The London Marathon is an almost unique occasion in that traffic and other hazards are directed around the runners.

Normally marathon runners have to go round hazards, although this is not alway possible if you suddenly find that miles 18 and 19 are now separated by a brand new six-lane motorway.

So this is merely a guide, not your official instructions. If a course description here includes a steep hill, well, there was a steep hill there last time I looked, but I can't guarantee that it won't have been bulldozed flat, tunnelled through, or circumnavigated before next year's race.

A Selection of UK Marathons

Aberdeen Milk Marathon. Organized by Aberdeen Amateur Athletic Club. Normally held in September. Convenor: Mel Edwards, 7 Middleton Terrace, Bridge of Don, Aberdeen AB2 8HY. 1981 entry fee: £1.00.

Starts and finishes at University Playing Fields Running Track, Balgownie Rd, Bridge of Don, Aberdeen.

Adidas British Marathon. Established 1981. Held in August. Organizer: Vince Regan, 424 St Helens Rd, Bolton, Lancashire.

Race starts from Deane Base Schools, Bolton (exit 5, M61 motorway), on a one-lap course on wide roads through highly populated areas, finishing in Bolton. No time or numerical limit on entry.

Barnsley Marathon. Established 1975. Organized by the Barnsley Road Runners Club. Normally held late November/early December. Organizer: Peter Gledhill, 9 Richard Rd, Darton, Barnsley, South Yorkshire. 1981 entry fee: 60p.

Out-and-back course, starting and finishing at Barnsley Town Hall. Mildly undulating, with a couple of stiff climbs between 20 and 24 miles. From 1981 a finishing limit of 4¼ hours was set, and anyone failing to pass 20 miles inside 3 hours is asked to retire from the race and get on the back-up bus. This is for safety reasons as, despite the 12 noon start, it gets dark very quickly by late afternoon.

Cambridge Marathon. Established 1980. Open to men over 40 and women only. Organized by Cambridge & Coleridge AC. Normally held in April. Organizer: Kevin St John Robinson, 12 Bateman St, Cambridge. 1981 entry fee: £1.00.

Competitors assemble at Long Road Sixth Form College, and

are transported by coach to the start at King's Parade, Route heads south for 2½ miles, then covers two laps of approximately 11 miles each (predominantly flat, with one stiff climb at Wandlebury) before heading back to Cambridge, and the finish at the college. Time limit of 4½ hours.

Cleveland County Marathon. Normally held in October. Organized by Cleveland Leisure Services, Education Offices, Woodlands Rd, Middlesbrough, Cleveland TS1 3BN, in conjunction with Middlesbrough and Cleveland Harriers.

Starts at Clairville Stadium, Middlesbrough, then leads into three laps of a flat anti-clockwise course, and finishing at the stadium. Not recommended for runners likely to take longer than 4 hours.

Duchy Marathon. Established 1977. Usually held in late March. Promoted by Duchy of Cornwall Athletic Club. Organizer: W. Dobson, Barton Farm, Blackwater, Truro, Cornwall TR4 8HY.

A point-to-point course, from Land's End to Redruth, and 'the toughest race I've ever run', according to 1981 winner Ian Thompson. It certainly ranks at least alongside the Isle of Wight race as the most challenging in Britain. The route starts at the road junction midway between Land's End and Sennen. The first 8 miles are undulating, with many short hills. The main gradients are at Leha (4M), Lower Drift (6M), and Beryas Bridge (7M). The road meanders, and runners must be careful on the bends. From 8–10 miles the course follows the main road through Penzance, and from 10–18 miles it is reasonably flat, except for a climb after leaving Crowlas (13M). The section from 18–22 miles is very hilly, with a long climb into Connor Downs (19M), and then a steep downhill, followed by a steep uphill at Roseworthy (20–21½M). The last 4 miles are reasonably flat, passing through Camborne, apart from a steep down and uphill at 24 miles. At 26 miles there is a left turn into the tree-lined drive of the Penventon Hotel at Redruth, with the finish line at the hotel itself.

Flying Fox Marathon: British Veteran Marathon Championship. Normally held in October. Organized by the Stone Master Marathoners, at Stone, Staffordshire. Organizer: Monica Darlington, The Radfords, Stone, Staffs ST15 8DJ. 1981 entry fee: £2.00.

Harlow Unigate Marathon. Established 1965. Normally held in late October. Promoted by Harlow Athletic Club. Organizer: Tom Dradey, 78 The Maples, Harlow, Essex CM19 4RA. 1981 entry fee: 75p.

The race starts at Harlow Sports Centre with two laps of the running track, followed by one small lap of approximately 4½ miles, and then two laps of 10¾ miles each. The course follows road and cycle paths within the New Town, and is undulating. The finish is on the large triangular concourse just outside the main sports centre gates. Time checks are given at 10, 20, 30 and 40 kilometres.

Horsforth May Day Metro Marathon. Established 1981. Held in early May. Promoted by Horsforth Sports Council. Organizer: Gerry Breakell, Area Community Education Officer, Horsforth School, Lee Lane East, Horsforth, Leeds LS18 5RF. 1981 entry fee: 50p.

Starts and finishes at Horsforth School, Leeds. Time limit of 5 hours.

Huddersfield Chippindale Marathon. Established 1968. Promoted by Longwood Harriers. Normally held in April. Organizer: John E. Sawyer, Shieling, 1 Ashfield Avenue, Skelmanthorpe, Huddersfield, HD8 9BW. 1981 entry fee: 75p.

Course starts and finishes at Leeds Road Playing Fields, Huddersfield, 2 miles from Town Centre, on main Huddersfield–Leeds road (A62), opposite ICI main gates. Route: Leeds Rd, St Andrews Rd, Firth St, Colne Rd, Folly Hall, Albert Rd, Lockwood, Berry Brow, Brockholes, New Mill, Holmfirth, Hagg Wood, Brockholes, New Mill, Holmfirth, Honley, Berry Brow, Lockwood, Albert Rd, Folly Hall, Colne Rd, Firth St, Apsley, Southgate and Leeds Rd. Time checks at 5, 10, 15 and 20 miles.

Isle of Man Open Marathon. Normally held in September. Organized by the Isle of Man Athletic Association. Flat course. Organizer: David W. Phillips, Flat 5, 89 Woodbourne Rd, Douglas, Isle of Man.

Isle of Wight Marathon. Established 1957. Normally held in May. Organized by Ryde Harriers. Organizer: John Symonds, Ryde Harriers HQ, 31 High St, Oakfield, Ryde, Isle of Wight PO33 1EJ. 1981 entry fee: £1.00.

This one-lap race has long been acknowledged as a tough, hilly circuit. It starts on the road opposite the Pavilion on Ryde Esplanade (adjacent to the pier and hovercraft terminal), heading in an easterly direction, covering two laps around the nearby Canoe Lake, and then back along the Esplanade and out via George St, Cross St, High St, John St, and Queens Rd. From there the circuit is anti-clockwise, on the eastern half of the island. The race passes through Binstead (3M), Wootton (5M), Binfield (8M), Newport (9M), Shide (9¾M), Blackwater (11M), Rookley (12M), the picturesque thatched-cottage village of Godshill (14½M), Sandford Nurseries (15M), Shanklin (18M), Lake (19M), Sandown (20M), Brading (22M), Elmfield (25M), and back to the finish at Ryde Esplanade. There are no time limits for the race, and certificates are awarded to all runners completing the course.

Jersey Coca-Cola Marathon. Established 1980. Held in early May. Organized by Jersey Spartan Athletic Club. Organizer: Patrick Tobin, 57 Don Farm, St Brelade, Jersey, Channel Islands. 1981 entry fee: 35p.

Starts at the Coca-Cola depot, Rue des Près Trading Estate. Two-lap clockwise course, reasonably flat, passing Le Boulivot, La Hogue Bie, Maufant, St Martin's Church, Gorey, La Rocque Point, Pontac and Dongueville. Certificates for all finishers under 4½ hours; no official times recorded after 4½ hours.

Leicester Charities Marathon. Normally held in September. Organized by Leicester Coritanian Athletic Club, supported by Leicester & Rutland AAA. Organizer: I.S. Davidson, Castles, Dover St, Church Gate, Leicester, LE1 3AJ. 1981 entry fee: £1.00.

London Marathon. Established 1981. Held in early May. Organized by the London Marathon Board of Governors. Race director: Chris Brasher, Gillette London Marathon, PO Box 82, County Hall, London SE1 7PE.

The course used for the inaugural London Marathon started in Greenwich, heading east, then doubled back on itself alongside the River Thames, through Lewisham and Southwark to cross the river at Tower Bridge. Then it headed east again to Tower Hamlets and around the Isle of Dogs, and back westwards through Wapping, the City, and on to the finish in Westminster.

The route was almost totally flat, starting at Charlton Way/
Greenwich Park, then on to Vanbrugh Park, Charlton Rd, Marl-
borough Rd, Canberra Rd, Charlton Park Lane, Repository Rd,
Frances St, Woolwich Church St, Woolwich Rd (4M), Trafalgar
Rd, Romney Rd, William Walk, Greenwich Church St, Creek Rd,
Creek Bridge, Evelyn St, Bestwood St, Bush Rd, Rotherhithe
New Road, Hawkstone Rd, Southwark Park, Lower Rd, Redriff
Rd (8½ M), Rotherhithe St, St Mary Church St, Jamaica Rd,
Tooley St, Tower Bridge Rd, crossing the Thames from south to
north at Tower Bridge (13M), the halfway mark.

Then, north of the river, the race turned east again, covering
Tower Bridge Approach, Mansell St, East Smithfield, The High-
way, Cannon St Rd, Cable St, Butcher Row, Commercial Rd,
West India Dock Rd, Ming St, Poplar High St (16M), Preston's
Rd, Manchester Rd, West Ferry Rd, Limehouse Causeway,
Narrow St, The Highway, Garnet St (21M), Wapping High St, St
Katharine's Way, St Katharine's Dock, The Tower of London,
Tower Hill, Lower Thames St, Upper Thames St, Blackfriars
Underpass (24M), Victoria Embankment, Bridge St, Parliament
Square, Great George St, Birdcage Walk (26M), Queen Vic-
toria's Monument, to the finish on Constitution Hill. From 1982
the finish has been switched to Westminster Bridge.

Milton Keynes International Marathon. Normally held in
July. Organized by the Road Runners Club and local athletics
clubs. Organizer: Ian Champion, 83 Fishponds Rd, Tooting,
London SW17 7LJ. 1981 entry fee: 50p for RRC Members; £1.00
for non-members. Time limit of 3 hours and 45 minutes.

Starts on Monk's Way, near the Stantonbury Centre, Milton
Keynes. There is a preliminary circuit of 2 miles, starting east-
wards along Monk's Way, before it joins the lap at the crossing of
the four Redway paths at the back of the Stantonbury Centre.
Then there are three anti-clockwise laps of approximately 8 miles
each, on undulating, traffic-free cycle paths.

Newcastle Marathon. Normally held in August. Organizer: Bill
Dewing, 19 Swaledale Gardens, Newcastle upon Tyne NE7 7TA.
1981 entry fee: 60p.

Starts in Etherstone Avenue, next to the Sports Pavilion of the
University of Newcastle, Coach Lane, Newcastle 7. Four com-

plete circuits of 6 miles 485 yards through the suburbs of Newcastle upon Tyne, plus extra distance to finish to make up correct length. Two short climbs on each lap. Time checks at 5, 10, 15 and 20 miles.

Newport (Gwent) Marathon. Normally held in August. Out-and-back course, covered four times. Organizer: J. Johnson, 26 Birch Hill, Newport NPT 6JD. 1981 entry fee: £1.00.

North Tyneside Marathon. Established 1979. Normally held in July. Organized by North Tyneside Metropolitan Borough Council, Town Hall, Wallsend, Tyne and Wear. 1981 entry fee: £1.00.

Starts and finishes at Whitley Bay Links, opposite the Spanish City, with a one-lap circuit through Hartley, Earsdon, Backworth, Camperdown, Wide Open, Seaton Burn, Dudley, Burradon, Killingworth Township, Forest Hall, Holystone, West Allotment, New York, Billy Mill, Cullercoats and back to Whitley Bay. The race for serious runners starts one hour ahead of a 'People's Marathon', open to joggers and runners alike, with every finisher under 6½ hours receiving a certificate.

Polytechnic Marathon. Established 1909. Normally held in June. Organized by Polytechnic Harriers. Organizer: Jack Micklewright MBE, 299 Jersey Rd, Osterley, Isleworth, Middlesex TW7 5PH. 1981 entry fee: £1.00.

The grandfather of the British marathon world. No longer the biggest, but still steeped in history and tradition: (the list of past winners on page 161 speaks for itself). More than half a dozen different routes have been used since 1909, all (apart from the Second World War years) starting from Windsor, and ending variously at Stamford Bridge, White City and Chiswick, before traffic problems led to the current route, adopted from 1973, which stays entirely in the vicinity of Windsor itself.

The race consists of one clockwise lap, finishing about a mile from the start. It begins in the private grounds of Windsor Castle, into which, for security reasons, only runners are allowed. Spectators can watch the start from Park Street, and the verges of the Long Walk.

The runners leave the castle through the George IV Gateway, and on to the Long Walk. They cross the A308 road at 1M, and continue to the Copper Horse (2¼M), turning right, then left after passing Sawmill and Farm (4M), and left before Sandpit Gate; they cross Queen Anne's Ride, pass Cumberland Lodge (6M), turn right at the T-junction, through Cumberland Gate (7M), past Smith's Lawn, Valley Gardens, and Johnson's Pond (7½M) to the first feeding station near Blacknest Gate. (The initial 7¾ miles in Windsor Great Park is prohibited to motor vehicles, but accessible throughout to the public on foot.)

The race moves on to public roads from Blacknest Gate, turning right out of the Park, along Mill Lane, right into the B383 (10M), past Ascot Gate, left into Woodside, then across the A332 at Crispin Inn into Lovel Lane (10¾M), left at Fleur de Lys crossroads to (11M) Brookside Autopoint (second feeding station). It forks right into Forest Road, right again (12½M) into Winkfield Row, right along the B3017 and right (13¼M) into the B3022. Left at Maiden's Green into A330 (14½M), and left at Malt Lane to the third feeding station. Right at Warfield Church and right at the next three junctions (17M), past Jealott's Hill, to the A330, then right and left (18M) to Nuptown (fourth feeding station).

Along Bishop's Lane, left into Winkfield Lane to Drift Road (20M), where the runners then turn left to the fifth feeding station at New Lodge Farm (21½M). Right to the B3383, right again through Oakley Green and right at Nags Head into Dedworth Road (sixth feeding station) leading into Clarence Road. They take the left hand subway at roundabout (25¼M) back into Clarence Road, right into Vansittart Road and right on to track at the Stadium. The race ends with 1¾ laps of the track, finishing opposite the clubhouse.

There is a time-limit for entry of 3 hours 20 minutes, or reasonably comparable performance in a long-distance race. Time certificates are awarded to all finishers.

Preston to Morecambe Marathon. Normally held in July. Organizer: Phillip Grime, 43 Slyne Rd, Skerton, Lancaster, Lancashire LA1 2JH. 1981 entry fee: 60p.

A point-to-point course which starts in Lytham Rd, Preston and finishes at the Leisure Park, Morecambe. Time certificates to all finishers.

Rotherham Marathon. Normally held in September. Organizer: David Haywood, 14 Whitehill Rd, Brinsworth, Rotherham, South Yorkshire. 1981 entry fee: £1.00.

Starts near Wickersley Roundabout, 2½ miles outside Rotherham. Buses shuttle the runners from Herringthorpe Stadium (10 minutes ride) to the start. Race route is through Thurcroft, then two 9-mile laps on a figure-of-eight type course, returning through Thurcroft. When reaching the starting point, the runners turn left for the final 2½ miles downhill to the finish at Herringthorpe Stadium. No time limits, and all standards of runner are welcome.

Rugby Midland Marathon. Organized by Rugby and District AC. Normally held in September. Organizer: Roy Humphries, 361 Dunchurch Rd, Rugby, Warwickshire. 1981 entry fee: £1.00.

Starts and finishes at Dunsmore Boys' School, Ashlawn Rd, Rugby. Three-lap course, with the first lap slightly shorter than the other two, but each involving a steep climb up Carthorse Hill. Pleasant country circuit, relatively light traffic. No official time-standard, but runners capable of breaking 4½ hours are preferred.

Sandbach Marathon. Established 1977. Normally held in June. Promoted by the Congleton Sports Council. Organizer: John Nolan, 7 Kendal Place, Clayton, Newcastle, Staffs ST5 3QT. 1981 entry fee: £1.00.

Starts close to, and finishes at, Sandbach Leisure Centre, Middlewich Rd, Sandbach, Cheshire. A three-lap anti-clockwise course over rural, flat, quiet country roads around Bradwall and Sproston. Acknowledged as one of the fastest courses in Britain. At the narrowest part of the oval-shaped lap there are several footpaths which enable spectators to go between both sides of the course. At the end of the third lap, the runners turn into the leisure centre for the finish. Certificates for all finishers.

Sandwell Marathon. Established 1981. Held in July. Organizer: Mick Lockwood, Haden Hill Leisure Centre, Barrs Rd, Cradley Heath, Warley, West Midlands.

Scottish Marathon. Normally held in June. Starts and finishes from Meadowbank Stadium, Edinburgh, with out-and-back course along the Firth of Forth to Granton, with a loop round Cramond. Fairly flat. Organizer: Colin Shields, 21 Bogton Avenue, Glasgow G44.

Wear Valley Marathon. Established 1981. Held early September. Organized by the Crook and District Sports and Athletic Club in association with Wear Valley District Council. Organizer: Lewis McEldon, Wear Valley District Council, Highfield, Crook, Co Durham. 1981 entry fee: £1.00.

The course is a point-to-point route, dropping 1000 feet from start to finish. Transport is provided from Crook to the starting point at Killhope Wheel (grid reference NY826429), elevation 1600 feet. The race descends via St John's Chapel, Stanhope, Wolsingham, and finishes at the Peases West Sports Centre, Crook (grid reference NZ163365), elevation 600 feet. Entry limited to 1000.

The following group of UK events are designed more for the fun runner than the serious competitor, and most of them are *not* held under AAA or WAAA Laws.

Alan Blatchford Masters and Maidens Marathon. Established 1975. Normally held in October. Organized by the MABAC Fun Run League. Event secretary: Roger Smith, 14 Amberwood Rise, New Malden, Surrey. 1981 entry fee: £1.50.

'The object of the event is to provide an opportunity for joggers and runners to attempt the traditional marathon distance of 26 miles 385 yards without having to enter a formal race. The distance may be covered by running, jogging or walking, but in the interests of safety there will be a time limit of 5½ hours in which to finish.

'Entry is open to all, irrespective of age or sex, except that entries from men aged between twenty and forty who have bettered 3 hours for the distance will not be accepted, unless they intend to accompany a member of their family on the run. Entry by people under twelve is not encouraged.'

This, the original marathon fun run, takes place south-west of Guildford, through a narrow but attractive course. Entry is limited to around 900 runners only on safety grounds. Steppingstone events of 10 miles (in July) and 15 miles (in September) are also held in Surrey, and organized by the MABAC Fun Run League.

Birmingham Nike People's Marathon. Established 1980.
Normally held in May. Organized by Centurion Joggers.
Organizer: John F. Walker, 111 Cooks Lane, Kingshurst, Bir-
mingham B37 6NU. 1981 entry fee: £2.50.

For the first two years it was staged at Chelmsley Wood,
Birmingham, over two laps of 13 miles, with only one hill and
three slight gradients each circuit. Limited to 2000 runners in
1981, with men who had bettered 2 hours 40 minutes in the
previous 16 months ineligible. But there are plans to switch the
event to the National Exhibition Centre in future, increasing the
entry limit to 5000.

Kingswood Festival Marathon. Established 1981. Held in May.
Promoted by Kingswood District Council, Bristol. Organizer:
P.J. Forward, Leisure Services Officer, Kingswood District
Council, Warmley House, Tower Road North, Warmley, Bristol
BS15 2XW. 1981 entry fee: £1.00.

Starts at Page Park, Staple Hill (on B4465, east of Bristol), and
passes through Mangotsfield, Rodway Common, Goose Green
and Webbs Heath.

Londonderry Radio Foyle Festival Marathon. Established
1981. Held early May. Organized by Londonderry City Council
in conjunction with Radio Foyle. Organizer: Liam Ball, 5 Guil-
dhall St, Londonderry, BT48 6BJ. 1981 entry fee: £1.50.

Starts and finishes at Templemore Sports Complex, Buncrana
Rd, Londonderry. The course is an out-and-back route, well over
90 per cent flat, with only one climb at approximately 14 miles. It
takes in both east and west banks of the River Foyle, crossing
Craigavon Bridge twice, and includes City centre, suburban and
rural areas. Certificates and medallions for all finishers.

Stockport Joggers and Walkers Marathon. Normally held in
May. Starts and finishes at the athletics track in Woodbank Park,
Stockport, and the course may be run, jogged or walked by
members of either sex, over sixteen on the day of the event. At
police request, the start is staggered, with twenty entrants leaving
every minute. In 1981 there was a limit of 800 entries, and the
entry fee of £1.50 went towards helping spastic adults and children. One lap course, with certificates to all who finish within 6
hours. Organizer: Brian Dowey, 7 Grosvenor Rd, Marple, Stockport, Cheshire SK6 6PR.

Further afield

The following section gives some examples of the many international marathons open to the globe-trotting runner, whether abroad on business or pleasure. In contacting the organizers of any of these races, it is advisable to enclose a self-addressed foolscap envelope and an international reply coupon.

If you intend to run in any race abroad, it is necessary to obtain the permission of the British Amateur Athletic Board (Francis House, Francis St, London SW1) in advance. Their permission is never unreasonably withheld, but the organizers of the race abroad may ask to see that permission before you can compete.

This list includes some of the leading races on the European and North American continents, but it is by no means complete.

Athens Open International Marathon. Normally held in October, and not to be confused with the Athens National Marathon in April, to which overseas athletes are sent by their national federations. The October race follows the same traditional course, but is open to all, with no qualifying times necessary. Buses take competitors to the start, near the Tomb of Marathon, and the course finishes in the white marble Olympic Stadium, near the centre of Athens. A hard course, often accompanied by hot and humid weather, but steeped in history. Contact: Athens Open International Marathon, 10 Panepistimiou Street, Athens 134, Greece.

Berlin Marathon. September. Race starts at the Reichstag (Platz der Republik), then winds through eight of the city's boroughs, and finishes at the Emperor William Memorial Church. All finishers within 5 hours receive a medal and certificate. Contact: Sport-Club Charlottenburg e.v., Berlin Marathon, Post Office Box 19 18 66, D-1000 Berlin 19, Germany.

Bermuda Marathon. Last Sunday in January. A particularly scenic race, starting 150 yards from the National Stadium, passing through the capital, Hamilton, alongside the ocean, and finishing inside the stadium. All participants receive certificates. A 10-km road race is held the day before the marathon. Contact: Bermuda Track and Field Association, PO Box 397, Bermuda.

Boston Marathon. Monday (Patriots Day) in late April. The oldest marathon in the USA, first held in 1897, and run from

Hopkinton virtually in a straight line to Boston, on a course which drops 500 feet overall from start to finish. The route goes through Ashland, Framingham, Natick, with the halfway point at Welles-ley, Newton, the infamous Heartbreak Hill (which is the last of a series of hills between 18–21 miles), past Boston College, and the final 5 downhill miles to the finishing line at the Prudential Centre in Boston. Buses transport the runners from Boston to the start. A minimum standard of entry was introduced to keep the numbers down to manageable levels. In 1982 these were 2 hours 50 minutes for men under forty, 3 hours 10 minutes for men forty to forty-nine, 3 hours 20 minutes for men fifty to fifty-nine, and 3 hours 30 minutes over sixty. For women, 3 hours 20 minutes under forty, and 3 hours 30 minutes over forty. Contact: Boston Athletic Association, PO Box 223, Boston, Massachusetts 02199, USA.

Copenhagen Marathon. June. The route covers an attractive part of North Copenhagen on a point to point course, starting in the city's Faelledparken, and finishing on the track of the Rund-forbi Stadium in Naerum. Buses transport the runners back afterwards. Time limit for the race is 6 hours, with a medal and T-shirt for all finishers. Contact: Copenhagen Marathon, Postbox 5, DK-2850 Naerum, Denmark.

Enschede Marathon. July. Biennial race first staged in 1947 in this Dutch town situated near the German border. An out-and-back course, starting and finishing at the town's Diekman Stadium. It was previously thought of more as an élite runners' event, but in 1981 was open to competitors with times up to 3 hours 45 minutes. Contact: The Secretary, Foundation Marathon Enschede, Dahliastraat 154, 7531 DS Enschede, Holland.

Essonne Marathon, Paris. Mid-March. One lap course, starting at Verrières le Buisson, and finishing at Massy, about 2 miles away. Time limit of 4½ hours; runners reaching the halfway point outside 2½ hours are asked to retire, and are taken by bus to the finish. Certificates are sent to all finishers after the race. Contact: M. Claude Noury, 3 rue Corvisart, F-91200 Athis-Mons, France.

Florida Orange Bowl Marathon. January. The course is out-and-back, flat, and starts and finishes inside the Miami Orange Bowl. The weather is often sunny and humid, ranging from 65° to

80° F. Contact: Rebecca Elks, Florida International University, Tamiami Trail, Room P C 230, Miami, Florida FL 33199 USA.

Frankfurt International Marathon. Mid-May. Flat, traffic-free course, through attractive parts of the city, and alongside the River Main. Contact: OSC Hoeschst Marathon Office, Postfach 80 06 45, D-6230 Frankfurt am Main 80, West Germany.

Helsinki City Marathon. Late July. Starts and finishes inside the 1952 Olympic Stadium.

Honolulu Marathon. Mid-December. Considered to be the third 'big' US marathon, alongside New York and Boston, and organized by the Honolulu Marathon Association. The course is scenic, beside the Pacific Ocean, and mostly flat, but with one slight hill. It begins at Aloha Tower and finishes at Kapiolani Park. The race starts at 6 a.m. to avoid the worst of the heat (usually in the low 80s F) and humidity. Contact: Honolulu Marathon Association, PO Box 27244, Chinatown Station, Honolulu, Hawaii, 96827, USA.

Letterkenny Marathon. Co Donegal. Course of 2½ laps of approximately 10 miles in and around Letterkenny. Flat course as it follows the River Swilly on its last phase to the sea at Lough Swilly. Finish at the Athletic Track, Railway Rd. Certificates to all finishers. Contact: Michael Cullen, 7 College Row, Letterkenny, Co Donegal, Eire.

Maryland Marathon. Baltimore. First Sunday in December. Course starts and finished at Baltimore Memorial Stadium, and consists of rolling hills and flats. Temperature usually 35° to 45° F. Contact: Maryland Marathon Commission, PO Box 11394B, Baltimore, Maryland 21239, USA.

Montreal International Marathon. Mid-September. The race starts on the Jacques Cartier Bridge, and is run through the city of Montreal in one large loop. Flat, it finishes on the Isle St Hélène, on the St Lawrence River. There were nearly 10,000 starters in 1980. Contact: Montreal International Marathon, PO Box 1570, Station B, Montreal, Canada H3B 3L2.

New Orleans Mardi Gras Marathon. Early February. The 'windy' race (see page 102), featuring the 24-mile long straight Lake Pontchartrain Causeway. Good fun if the wind is blowing the right way. Contact: George De Dual, 6034 Catina St, New Orleans, Louisiana 70124, USA.

New York City Marathon. Late October. First held in 1970, and now probably the most famous marathon in the world. Starts at the Toll Plaza on Staten Island, crosses the Verrazano Bridge into Brooklyn, touring all five New York boroughs. There are checkpoints in Brooklyn at 5M (4th Avenue and 45th St) and 10M (Bedford and Flushing), in Queens at the half-distance (Pulaski Bridge) and 15M (Queensboro Bridge), in the Bronx at 20M (Willis Ave Bridge and 135th St), and in Manhattan at 25M (East Park Drive and 66th St), before the finish at the Tavern on the Green restaurant in Central Park. Mainly flat.

No time limit for entries, but demand far exceeds available places; a good approach may be through one of the organized tours from the UK which can often arrange your entry too. For inquiries contact New York Road Runners Club, Box 881, FDR Station, New York, New York 10022, USA. To apply for an entry form send a 4¼ × 9½ inch self-addressed envelope and an international reply coupon (but enclose no letters) to NYRRC Marathon Entries, PO Box 1388 GPO, New York, NY 10001, USA, ensuring that it is postmarked no *earlier* than 2 June in the year you wish to compete.

Oslo Marathon. July. Starts in front of the Town Hall, and finishes on the track in the city's famous Bislett Stadium.

Ottawa National Capital Marathon. May. Out-and-back course follows paved, traffic-free parkways, and is run on some rolling terrain, beginning and ending at the Carleton University Physical Recreation Centre. Contact: National Capital Marathon, PO Box 426, Postal Station 'A', Ottawa, Ontario, Canada K1N 8V5.

Paris Marathon. Late May. Starts at the Place du Trocadéro, and passes through the Bois de Boulogne, along the North Bank of the Seine, around the Bois de Vincennes, and back along the opposite side of the river, to finish just past the Eiffel Tower at the Pont d'Iéna. Time limit is 4½ hours. Contact: Marathon de Paris, 23 Rue de la Sourdière, 3ème étage, 75001 Paris, France.

San Francisco Marathon. July. Starts and ends in the Golden Gate Stadium, with a course through Golden Gate Park, alongside the Pacific Ocean, around Lake Merced, and back into the park; moderate hills. Weather is generally cool and foggy (7 a.m. start). Contact: Scott Thomason, 110 Lenox Way, San Francisco, California 94127, USA.

Sea of Galilee Marathon. Early January. Around the Biblical Lake, and the only marathon to be run below sea level. Commemorative medal and certificate to all finishers. Contact: Marathon Organizing Committee, Sports Federation of Israel, PO Box 4575, 4 Marmorek St, Tel Aviv, Israel.

Seattle Marathon. Late November. Starting and finishing in Seward Park, the course consists of two loops on a flat course along the shore of Lake Washington. Weather is usually cool and rainy, +40° F. Contact: Laurel James, Super Jock and Jill, 7210 East Greenlake Drive North, Seattle, Washington 98115, USA.

Stockholm Marathon. Mid-August. Mainly flat two-lap course through the centre of Stockholm, passing the city's landmarks, and along the waterways, to finish on the track of the stadium built for the 1912 Olympics. Entry limit of 7500 in 1981. Commemorative medal to all runners finishing inside 5 hours. Contact: Stockholm Marathon, Box 10023, S-100 55 Stockholm, Sweden.

Toronto Marathon. Early October. The flat course begins at Toronto City Hall and finishes at Varsity Stadium. Temperature ranges from 42° to 64° F. Contact: Race Secretary, 34 Mould Avenue, Toronto, Canada M6N 379.

Vancouver International Marathon. Early May. The course includes two laps of the scenic Stanley Park on paved roads, and begins and ends at Robson Square (7.30 a.m. start). Contact: Don Basham, Vancouver International Marathon, 1200 Hornby St, Vancouver, British Columbia, Canada V62 2E2.

9

Clubs and the Clock

Apart from the range of athletics clubs in the UK which operate mainly on a local geographical basis and cover all events, there are also a number of specialist distance running clubs of which membership is an addition rather than an alternative, but which can provide specific running information and advice not always available through the average athletics club:

The Road Runners Club (Hon. General Secretary: W.D. Turner, 40 Rosedale Road, Stoneleigh, Epsom, Surrey KT17 2JH) was founded in 1952, initially to organize its own annual London to Brighton 53½-mile road race, but its activities have since broadened considerably to span the whole range of distances from 10 miles upwards. Its current membership is around 3000, and its aim is 'to bring together all those interested in long distance running, to serve their interests, and to act as a forum for all enthusiasts'. It is open to membership by athletes belonging to clubs affiliated to the AAA or Women's AAA, and its activities include the publication of a high standard triennial newsletter, the operating of an accident insurance scheme covering any member injured or killed while training or racing in the UK, organizing film shows, maintaining a close surveillance on course measurement, and promoting a select number of its own races, including the London to Brighton, an annual marathon championship (usually at Milton Keynes in July) and a long distance autumn track race for élite runners.

It also operates a standards scheme for members which gives particular encouragement to those who do not normally expect to be among the prize-winners. Any RRC member who achieves a performance bettering the listed first- or second-class standards at three different distances of 10 miles and over within one year (calculated from 1 November to 31 October) is entitled to a certificate, which is sent without charge after the performances have been checked. The runner can also purchase a standard badge.

The standards are adjusted for various races to allow for any slight over-distance, a hilly course, and so forth, so that the standards are all of equal difficulty as far as can be judged. Slight amendments, as deemed necessary, are made from time to time, and races at 'odd' distances have standards calculated to the equivalent level.

There are separate schemes for veterans over forty and over fifty, and also for women, although in view of the more restricted number of races available for them at present, they are allowed to count two performances at the same distance towards their certificate. The full range of standards is published in the *RRC Newsletter*, together with additions and amendments, but the following list of standards for some of the UK marathons listed in chapter 8 will serve to illustrate the scheme:

			Men		*Women*	
	1st C	*2nd C*	*Vet 40*	*Vet 50*	*1st C*	*2nd C*
Aberdeen Marathon	2:37	3:07	3:12	3:27	3:12	3:44
Barnsley Marathon	2:35	3:05	3:10	3:25	3:05	3:42
Cambridge Marathon	—	—	3:10	3:25	3:05	3:42
Cleveland County Marathon	2:35	3:05	3:10	3:25	3:05	3:42
Duchy Marathon	2:39	3:09	3:14	3:29	3:09	3:46
Harlow Marathon	2:36	3:06	3:11	3:26	3:06	3:43
Huddersfield Marathon	2:35	3:05	3:10	3:25	3:05	3:42
Isle of Man Marathon	2:35	3:05	3:10	3:25	—	—
Ise of Wight Marathon	2:39	3:09	3:14	3:29	3:09	3:46
London Marathon ('81 course)	2:35	3:05	3:10	3:25	3:05	3:40
Milton Keynes Marathon	2:36	3:06	3:10	3:25	3:06	3:41
Newcastle Marathon	2:37	3:07	3:12	3:27	3:07	3:44
Newport Marathon	2:35	3:05	3:10	3:25	3:05	3:42
North Tyneside Marathon	2:35	3:05	3:10	3:25	3:05	3:42
Polytechnic Marathon	2:36	3:06	3:11	3:26	3:06	3:41
Preston–Morecambe Marathon	2:35	3:05	3:10	3:25	3:05	3:40
Rotherham Marathon	2:36	3:06	3:11	3:26	3:06	3:42
Rugby Marathon	2:37	3:07	3:12	3:27	3:07	3:42
Sandbach Marathon	2:35	3:05	3:10	3:23	3:05	3:40
Scottish Marathon	2:35	3:05	3:10	3:25	—	—

The British Marathon Runners Club (Hon. secretary: Terry Lewins, 13 Albany Rd, Old Windsor, Berkshire) was founded in 1978 'to raise the standard of British marathon running, improve the knowledge of coaches and runners, and to ensure that full advantage is taken of the international competition offered by other countries'.

Membership to athletes is restricted to a time-qualification, although the limits were eased at the club's 1981 annual meeting. Now men under forty who have bettered 3 hours, and women who have beaten 3½ hours, are eligible, with the following sub-categories of membership: (Men) Elite class – 2:20; First class – 2:30; Second class – 2:45; (Women) Elite class – 2:50; First class – 3:05; Second class – 3:30. The various benefits of membership increase according to the standard reached.

Additionally, there are Veteran standards for membership: (Men) 40–49: 3:15; 50–59: 3:40; 60 and over: 4:00; (Women) 35–49: 3:30; 50 and over: 4:00.

The Club organizes coaching days and seminars to help prospective coaches, and qualified BAAB Club coaches and others with specific qualities of benefit to the club are also eligible to join.

The London Road Runners Club (c/o 6 Upper Montagu St, London W1) is modelled on the New York City Road Runners Club, and was founded in 1981 by a group of active runners and coaches. It has the aim of providing a service for runners of all abilities and ages in the capital, including lectures, fixture lists, a newsletter, training and injury-treatment advice, the promotion of its own running events, and advice on the staging of anything from a fun run to a marathon.

The Scottish Marathon Club (Hon. Secretary: Gavin McKirdy, 55 Dunedin Drive, Hairmyres, East Kilbride, G75 8QF) was established to promote long-distance running events up to the marathon in Scotland. It imposes no time-qualifications for membership, and organizes its own championship based on selected races from 12–26 miles.

Pace Chart

The pace chart on page 148 shows in its extreme left-hand column a range of average miling paces from 4:45 to 10:00, and in the extreme right-hand column the final marathon time if that pace were kept up all the way through the race. In between are the intermediate times at 5, 10, 15 and 20 miles at that pace, although it is important to remember that most marathon runners slow in the latter stages of the race.

1 Mile Pace	5 Miles	10 km (6.2M)	15 km (9.3M)	10 Miles	20 km (12.4M)	Halfway (13.1M)	15 Miles	25 km (15.5M)	30 km (18.6M)	20 Miles	40 km (24.8M)	Full Marathon
4.45	23:45	29:27	44:11	47:30	58:54	1:02:16	1:11:15	1:13:38	1:28:21	1:35:00	1:57:48	2:04:33
4.50	24:10			48:20			1:12:30			1:36:40		2:07:44
5.00	25:00	31:00	46:30	50:00	1:02:00	1:05:33	1:15:00	1:17:30	1:33:00	1:40:00	2:04:00	2:11:06
5.10	25:50			51:40			1:17:30			1:43:20		2:15:28
5.15	26:15	32:33	48:50	52:30	1:05:06	1:08:50	1:18:45	1:21:23	1:37:39	1:45:00	2:10:12	2:17:40
5.20	26:40			53:20			1:20:00			1:46:50		2:19:50
5.30	27:30	34:06	51:09	55:00	1:08:12	1:12:07	1:22:30	1:25:15	1:42:18	1:50:00	2:16:24	2:24:12
5.40	28:20			56:40			1:25:00			1:53:20		2:28:34
5.45	28:45	35:39	53:29	57:30	1:11:18	1:15:23	1:26:15	1:29:08	1:46:57	1:55:00	2:22:36	2:30:46
5.50	29:10			58:20			1:27:30			1:56:40		2:32:56
6.00	30:00	37:12	55:48	1:00:00	1:14:24	1:18:39	1:30:00	1:33:00	1:51:36	2:00:00	2:28:48	2:37:19
6.10	30:50			1:01:40			1:32:30			2:03:20		2:41:41
6.15	31:15	38:45	58:08	1:02:30	1:17:30	1:21:56	1:33:45	1:36:53	1:55:45	2:05:00	2:35:00	2:43:53

1 Mile Pace	5 Miles	10 km (6.2M)	15 km (9.3M)	10 Miles	20 km (12.4M)	Halfway (13.1M)	15 Miles	25 km (15.5M)	30 km (18.6M)	20 Miles	40 km (24.8M)	Full Marathon
6.20	31:40			1:03:20			1:35:00			2:06:40		2:46:03
6.30	32:30	40:18	1:00:27	1:05:00	1:20:36	1:25:13	1:37:30	1:40:45	2:00:44	2:10:00	2:41:12	2:50:25
6.40	33:20			1:06:40			1:40:00			2:13:20		2:54:47
6.45	33:45	41:51	1:02:47	1:07:30	1:23:42	1:28:29	1:41:15	1:44:38	2:05:33	2:15:00	2:47:24	2:56:59
6.50	34:10			1:08:20			1:42:30			2:16:40		2:59:09
7.00	35:00	43:24	1:05:06	1:10:00	1:26:50	1:31:46	1:45:00	1:48:30	2:10:12	2:20:00	2:53:40	3:03:33
7.10	35:50			1:11:40			1:47:30			2:23:20		3:07:55
7.15	36:15	44:57	1:07:26	1:12:30	1:29:54	1:35:03	1:48:45	1:52:23	2:14:51	2:25:00	2:59:48	3:10:06
7.20	36:40			1:13:20			1:50:00			2:26:40		3:12:17
7.30	37:30	46:30	1:09:45	1:15:00	1:33:00	1:38:19	1:52:30	1:56:15	2:19:20	2:30:00	3:06:00	3:16:39
7.40	38:20			1:16:40			1:55:00			2:33:20		3:21:01
7.45	38:45	48:03	1:12:05	1:17:30	1:36:06	1:41:36	1:56:15	2:00:08	2:24:09	2:35:00	3:12:12	3:23:13
7.50	39:10			1:18:20			1:57:30			2:36:40		3:25:23

1 Mile Pace	5 Miles	10 km (6.2M)	15 km (9.3M)	10 Miles	20 km (12.4M)	Halfway (13.1M)	15 Miles	25 km (15.5M)	30 km (18.6M)	20 Miles	40 km (24.8M)	Full Marathon
8.00	40:00	49:36	1:14:24	1:20:00	1:39:12	1:44:53	2:00:00	2:04:00	2:28:48	2:40:00	3:18:24	3:29:45
8.10	40:50			1:21:40			2:02:30				2:43:20		3:34:07
8.15	41:15	51:09	1:16:44	1:22:30	1:42:12	1:48:10	2:03:45	2:07:53	2:33:27	2:45:00	3:24:24	3:36:20
8.20	41:40			1:23:20			2:05:00				2:46:40		3:38:29
8.30	42:30	52:42	1:19:03	1:25:00	1:45:24	1:51:26	2:07:30	2:11:45	2:38:06	2:50:00	3:30:48	3:42:51
8.40	43:20			1:26:40			2:10:00				2:53:20		3:47:13
8.45	43:45	54:15	1:21:23	1:27:30	1:48:30	1:54:43	2:11:15	2:15:38	2:42:45	2:55:00	3:37:00	3:49:26
8.50	44:10			1:28:20			2:12:30				2:56:40		3:51:35
9.00	45:00	55:48	1:23:42	1:30:00	1:51:36	1:57:59	2:15:00	2:19:30	2:47:24	3:00:00	3:43:12	3:56:00
9.10	45:50			1:31:40			2:17:30				3:03:20		4:00:22
9.15	46:15	57:21	1:26:02	1:32:30	1:54:42	2:01:16	2:18:45	2:23:23	2:52:03	3:05:00	3:49:24	4:02:32
9.20	46:40			1:33:20			2:20:00				3:06:40		4:04:44
9.30	47:30	58:54	1:28:21	1:35:00	1:57:48	2:04:33	2:22:30	2:27:15	2:56:42	3:10:00	3:55:36	4:09:06

1 Mile Pace	5 Miles	10 km (6.2M)	15 km (9.3M)	10 Miles	20 km (12.4M)	Halfway (13.1M)	15 Miles	25 km (15.5M)	30 km (18.6M)	20 Miles	40 km (24.8M)	Full Marathon
9.40	48:20			1:36:40			2:25:00			3:13:20		4:13:28
9.45	48:45	1:00:27	1:30:41	1:37:30	2:00:54	2:07:49	2:26:15	2:31:08	3:01:21	3:15:00	4:01:48	4:15:33
9.50	49:10			1:38:20			2:27:30			3:16:40		4:17:50
10.00	50:00	1:02:00	1:33:00	1:40:00	2:04:00	2:11:06	2:30:00	2:35:00	3:06:00	3:20:00	4:08:00	4:22:13

For the benefit of those running in Europe, or in one of the races where time 'splits' are now given at kilometre- rather than mile-points, some representative times for the same miling-pace at 10, 15, 20, 25, 30 and 40 km are also shown as a guide, as well as 'halfway' times.

Runners who wish to follow a time-schedule closely often write down their planned schedule on their hand or arm in ball-point pen; beware if you use felt-tipped pen, though: one quick rain shower, and you'll be left with just a smudge!

Last Word

With the marathon boom has come the outbreak of a new condition which I call the Seven Mile Itch. It usually comes when a runner in training for his first marathon reaches a level of fitness where he can run 7 miles in something around an hour. It seems a long way, and a lot of progress to have made, and it usually is. But then he starts thinking about the remaining 19 miles, which seem one hell of a distance still to run, and he starts looking around to find a new model of shoe, a new kind of food, or a different type of training which will help him reach his goal more quickly.

Unfortunately, there are no short cuts. But what you can look forward to is that, as you get fitter, so the momentum speeds up. Increasing your longest-ever run from, say, 17 to 19 miles is much easier than going from 3 to 5 miles, because the jump is becoming a much smaller percentage of the whole. It is like getting a car moving. You need all the power of the first and second gears at the start, but once you are rolling, it's much easier to progress.

In a marathon, it's never actually easy, and 26 miles is a long way. But if it *were* easy, there would be little point to it, would there? And you certainly wouldn't feel the sense of deep satisfaction and pride which awaits you when you can finally run the distance. For, after all, that's the Challenge of the Marathon.

Appendix I

Records and Winners

The marathon is steeped in history, and this section records the names of the men and women who created that history, and who pushed back the frontiers of what was thought possible for the human body in terms of running endurance.

In chronological order, here are the world and UK 'best performances' (in view of the differing terrain of the courses, no official records are ratified for the marathon), the medallists in Olympic, European and Commonwealth Games marathons, and the roll of winners in some of the world's most prestigious marathons.

(*NB: In accordance with current international ruling, times originally recorded to a tenth of a second have been rounded up to the nearest full second.*)

World's Best Progression – Men

2:55.19	John Hayes (USA)	Windsor–Shepherd's Bush	24 July 1908
2:52.46	Robert Fowler (USA)	Yonkers, New York	1 Jan. 1909
2:46.53	James Clark (USA)	New York	12 Feb. 1909
2:46.05	Albert Raines (USA)	New York	8 May 1909
2:42.31	Fred Barrett (Gt Britain)	Windsor–Stamford Bridge	26 May 1909
2:38.17	Harry Green (Gt Britain)	Shepherd's Bush	12 May 1913
2:36.07	Alexis Ahlgren (Sweden)	Windsor–Stamford Bridge	31 May 1913
2:32.36	Hannes Kolehmainen (Finland)	Antwerp	22 Aug. 1920
2:29.02	Albert Michelsen (USA)	Port Chester	12 Oct. 1925
2:27.49	Fusashige Suzuki (Japan)	Tokyo	31 March 1935
2:26.44	Yasuo Ikenaka (Japan)	Tokyo	3 April 1935
2:26.42	Kitei Son (Japan)	Tokyo	3 Nov. 1935
2:25.39	Yun Bok Suh (Korea)	Boston	19 April 1947
2:20.43	Jim Peters (Gt Britain)	Windsor–Chiswick	14 June 1952
2:18.41	Jim Peters (Gt Britain)	Windsor–Chiswick	13 June 1953

2:18.35	Jim Peters (Gt Britain)	Turku	4 Oct. 1953
2:17.40	Jim Peters (Gt Britain)	Windsor–Chiswick	26 June 1954
2:15.17	Sergei Popov (USSR)	Stockholm	24 Aug. 1958
2:15.17	Abebe Bikila (Ethiopia)	Rome	10 Sep. 1960
2:15.16	Toru Terasawa (Japan)	Beppu	17 Feb. 1963
2:14.28	Buddy Edelen (USA)	Windsor–Chiswick	15 June 1963
2:13.55	Basil Heatley (Gt Britain)	Windsor–Chiswick	13 June 1964
2:12.12	Abebe Bikila (Ethiopia)	Tokyo	21 Oct. 1964
2:12.00	Morio Shigematsu (Japan)	Windsor–Chiswick	12 June 1965
2:09.37	Derek Clayton (Australia)	Fukuoka	3 Dec. 1967
2:08.34	Derek Clayton (Australia)	Antwerp	30 May 1969
2:08.13	Alberto Salazar (USA)	New York	25 Oct. 1981

World's Best Progression – Women

3:37.07	Merry Lepper (USA)	Culver City	14 Dec. 1963
3:27.45	Dale Greig (Gt Britain)	Ryde, Isle of Wight	23 May 1964
3:19.33	Millie Sampson (New Zealand)	Auckland	21 July 1964
3:15.22	Maureen Wilton (Canada)	Toronto	8 May 1967
3:07.26	Anni Pede-Erdkamp (West Germany)	Waldniel	16 Sep. 1967
3:02.53	Caroline Walker (USA)	Seaside, Oregon	28 Feb. 1970
3:01.42	Beth Bonner (USA)	Philadelphia	9 May 1971
3:00.35	Sara Berman (USA)	Brockton, Massachusetts	30 May 1971
2:55.22	Beth Bonner (USA)	New York	19 Sep. 1971
2:49.40	Cheryl Bridges (USA)	Culver City	5 Dec. 1971
2:46.36	Miki Gorman (USA)	Culver City	2 Dec. 1973
2:46.24	Chantal Langlace (France)	Neuf Brisach	27 Oct. 1974
2:43.54	Jackie Hansen (USA)	Culver City	1 Dec. 1974
2:42.24	Liane Winter (West Germany)	Boston	19 April 1975
2:40.15	Christa Vahlensieck (West Germany)	Dulmen	3 May 1975
2:38.19	Jackie Hansen (USA)	Eugene	12 Oct. 1975
2:35.16	Chantal Langlace (France)	San Sebastian	1 May 1977
2:34.48	Christa Vahlensieck (West Germany)	West Berlin	10 Sep. 1977
2:32.30	Grete Waitz (Norway)	New York	22 Oct. 1978
2:27.33	Grete Waitz (Norway)	New York	21 Oct. 1979
2:25.42	Grete Waitz (Norway)	New York	26 Oct. 1980
2:25.29	Allison Roe (NZ)	New York	25 Oct. 1981
2:25.29	Grete Waitz (Norway)	London	17 April 1983
2:22.43	Joan Benoit (USA)	Boston	18 April 1983

UK Best Progression – Men

2:42.31	Fred Barrett	Windsor–Stamford Bridge	26 May 1909
2:38.17	Harry Green	Shepherd's Bush (track!)	12 May 1913
2:37.41	Arthur Mills	Windsor–Stamford Bridge	17 July 1920
2:35.59	Sam Ferris	Windsor–Stamford Bridge	30 May 1925
2:35.27	Sam Ferris	Liverpool	28 Sep. 1927
2:34.34	Harry Payne	Windsor–Stamford Bridge	6 July 1928
2:33.00	Sam Ferris	Liverpool	26 Sep. 1928
2:30.58	Harry Payne	Windsor–Stamford Bridge	5 July 1929
2:29.28	Jim Peters	Windsor–Chiswick	16 June 1951
2:20.43	Jim Peters	Windsor–Chiswick	14 June 1952
2:18.41	Jim Peters	Windsor–Chiswick	13 June 1953
2:18.35	Jim Peters	Turku	4 Oct. 1953
2:17.40	Jim Peters	Windsor–Chiswick	26 June 1954
2:14.43	Brian Kilby	Port Talbot	6 July 1963
2:13.55	Basil Heatley	Windsor–Chiswick	13 June 1964
2:13.45	Alastair Wood	Inverness–Forres	9 July 1966
2:12.17	Bill Adcocks	Karl Marx Stadt	19 May 1968
2:10.48	Bill Adcocks	Fukuoka	8 Dec. 1968
2:10.30	Ron Hill	Hopkinton–Boston	20 April 1970
2:09.28	Ron Hill	Edinburgh	23 July 1970
2:09.12	Ian Thompson	Christchurch, New Zealand	31 Jan. 1974
2:09.08	Geoff Smith	New York	23 Oct. 1983

UK Best Progression – Women

3:27.45	Dale Greig	Ryde, Isle of Wight	23 May 1964
3:11.54	Anne Clarke	Guildford	19 Oct. 1975
3:07.47	Margaret Thompson	Korso, Finland	26 Oct. 1975
2:50.55	Christine Readdy	Feltham	16 April 1976
2:50.54	Rosemary Cox	Rugby	3 Sep. 1978
2:41.37	Joyce Smith	Sandbach	17 June 1979
2:41.03	Gillian Adams	Eugene	9 Sep. 1979
2:36.27	Joyce Smith	Waldniel, West Germany	22 Sep. 1979
2:33.32	Joyce Smith	Sandbach	22 June 1980
2:30.27	Joyce Smith	Tokyo	16 Nov. 1980
2:29.57	Joyce Smith	London	29 March 1981
2:29.43	Joyce Smith	London	9 May 1982

Olympic Marathon Medallists

	1	2	3
1896 Athens (40 km)	Spiridon Louis (Gre) 2:58.50	Harilaos Vasilakos (Gre) 3:06.03	Gyula Kellner (Hun) 3:06.35
1900 Paris (40.26 km)	Michel Theato (Fra) 2:59.45	Emile Champion (Fra) 3:04.17	Ernst Fast (Swe) 3:37.14
1904 St Louis (40 km)	Tom Hicks (USA) 3:28.53	Albert Corey (USA) 3:34.52	Arthur Newton (USA) 3:47.33
1908 London	Johnny Hayes (USA) 2:55.19	Charles Hefferon (USA) 2.56.06	Joseph Forshaw (USA) 2:57.11
1912 Stockholm (40.20 km)	Kenneth McArthur (SAf) 2:36.55	Chris Gitsham (SAf) 2:37.52	Gaston Strobina (USA) 2:38.43
1920 Antwerp (42.75 km)	Hannes Kolehmainen (Fin) 2:32.36	Juri Lossmann (Est) 2:32.49	Valerio Arri (Ita) 2:36.33
1924 Paris	Albin Stenroos (Fin) 2:41.23	Romeo Bertini (Ita) 2:47.20	Clarence DeMar (USA) 2:48.14
1928 Amsterdam	Boughera El Ouafi (Fra) 2:32.58	Manuel Plaza (Chile) 2:33.23	Martti Marttelin (Fin) 2:35.02
1932 Los Angeles	Juan Carlos Zabala (Arg) 2:31.36	Sam Ferris (GB) 2:31.55	Armas Toivonen (Fin) 2:32.12
1936 Berlin	Kitei Son (Jap) 2:29.20	Ernie Harper (GB) 2:31.24	Shoryu Nan (Jap) 2:31.42

Year	1	2	3
1948 London	Delfo Cabrera (Arg) 2:34.52	Tom Richards (GB) 2:35.08	Etienne Gailly (Bel) 2:35.34
1952 Helsinki	Emil Zatopek (Cze) 2:23.04	Reinaldo Gorno (Arg) 2:25.35	Gustaf Jansson (Swe) 2:26.07
1956 Melbourne	Alain Mimoun (Fra) 2:25.00	Franjo Mihalic (Yug) 2:26.32	Veikko Karvonen (Fin) 2:27.47
1960 Rome	Abebe Bikila (Eth) 2:15.17	Rhadi ben Abdesselem (Mor) 2:15.42	Barry Magee (NZ) 2:17.19
1964 Tokyo	Abebe Bikila (Eth) 2:12.12	Basil Heatley (GB) 2:16.20	Kokichi Tsuburaya (Jap) 2:16.23
1968 Mexico City	Mamo Wolde (Eth) 2:20.27	Kenji Kimihara (Jap) 2:23.31	Mike Ryan (NZ) 2:23.45
1972 Munich	Frank Shorter (USA) 2:12.20	Karel Lismont (Bel) 2:14.32	Mamo Wolde (Eth) 2:15.09
1976 Montreal	Waldemar Cierpinski (EG) 2:09.55	Frank Shorter (USA) 2:10.46	Karel Lismont (Bel) 2:11.13
1980 Moscow	Waldemar Cierpinski (EG) 2:11.03	Gerard Nijboer (Hol) 2:11.20	Setymkul Dzhumanazarov (USSR) 2:11.35

European Championship Medallists

Year	1	2	3
1934 Turin	Armas Toivonen (Fin) 2:52.29	Thore Enochsson (Swe) 2:54.36	Aurelio Genghini (Ita) 2:55.04
1938 Paris	Vaino Muinonen (Fin) 2:37.29	Squire Yarrow (GB) 2:39.03	Henry Palme (Swe) 2:42.14
1946 Oslo	Mikko Hietanen (Fin) 2:24.55	Vaino Muinonen (Fin) 2:26.08	Yakov Punko (USSR) 2:26.21

European Championship Medallists contd.

	1	2	3
1950 Brussels	Jack Holden (GB) 2:32.14	Veikko Karvonen (Fin) 2:32.46	Feodosiy Vanin (USSR) 2:33.47
1954 Berne	Veikko Karvonen (Fin) 2:24.52	Boris Grishayev (USSR) 2:24.56	Ivan Filin (USSR) 2:25.27
1958 Stockholm	Sergei Popov (USSR) 2:15.17	Ivan Filin (USSR) 2:20.51	Fred Norris (GB) 2:21.15
1962 Belgrade	Brian Kilby (GB) 2:23.19	Aurele Vandendriessche (Bel) 2:24.02	Viktor Baikov (USSR) 2:24.20
1966 Budapest	Jim Hogan (GB) 2:20.05	Aurele Vandendriessche (Bel) 2:21.44	Gyula Toth (Hun) 2:22.02
1969 Athens	Ron Hill (GB) 2:16.48	Gaston Roelants (Bel) 2:17.23	Jim Alder (GB) 2:19.06
1971 Helsinki	Karel Lismont (Bel) 2:13.09	Trevor Wright (GB) 2:14.00	Ron Hill (GB) 2:14.35
1974 Rome	Ian Thompson (GB) 2:13.19	Eckhard Lesse (EG) 2:14.58	Gaston Roelants (Bel) 2:16.30
1978 Prague	Leonid Moseyev (USSR) 2:11.58	Nikolay Penzin (USSR) 2:11.59	Karel Lismont (Bel) 2:12.08
1982 Athens	Gerard Nijboer (Hol) 2:15.17	Armand Parmentier (Bel) 2:15.40	Karel Lismont (Bel) 2:16.07

Commonwealth Games Medallists

Year / Venue	1	2	3
1930 Hamilton, Can	Dunky Wright (Sco) 2:43.43	Sam Ferris (Eng) (880 yd down)	John Miles (Can) (300 yd down)
1934 London	Harold Webster (Can) 2:40.36	Donald McNab Robertson (Sco) 2:45.08	Dunky Wright (Sco) 2:56.20
1938 Sydney	Johannes Coleman (SAf) 2:30.50	Bert Norris (Eng) 2:37.57	Henry Gibson (SAf) 2:38.20
1950 Auckland	Jack Holden (Eng) 2:32.57	Sydney Luyt (SAf) 2:37.03	Jack Clarke (NZ) 2:39.27
1954 Vancouver	Joe McGhee (Sco) 2:39.36	Jackie Mekler (SAf) 2:40.57	Johannes Barnard (SAf) 2:22.58
1958 Cardiff	Dave Power (Aus) 2:22.46	Johannes Barnard (SAf) 2:22.58	Peter Wilkinson (Eng) 2:24.42
1962 Perth, Aus	Brian Kilby (Eng) 2:21.17	Dave Power (Aus) 2:22.16	Rodney Bonella (Aus) 2:24.07
1966 Kingston, Jam	Jim Alder (Sco) 2:22.08	Bill Adcocks (Eng) 2:22.13	Mike Ryan (NZ) 2:27.59
1970 Edinburgh	Ron Hill (Eng) 2:09.28	Jim Alder (Sco) 2:12.04	Don Faircloth (Eng) 2:12.19
1974 Christchurch, NZ	Ian Thompson (Eng) 2:09.12	Jack Foster (NZ) 2:11.19	Richard Mabuza (Swaz) 2:12.55
1978 Edmonton, Can	Gidamis Shahanga (Tan) 2:15.40	Jerome Drayton (Can) 2:16.14	Paul Bannon (Can) 2:16.52
1982 Brisbane, Aus	Robert de Castella (Aus) 2:09.18	Juma Ikangaa (Tan) 2:09.30	Mike Gratton (Eng) 2:12.06

AAA Marathon Champions

				Venue
1925	Sam Ferris	(RAF)	2:35.59	Windsor–Stamford Bridge
1926	Sam Ferris	(RAF)	2:42.25	Windsor–Stamford Bridge
1927	Sam Ferris	(RAF)	2:40.33	Windsor–Stamford Bridge
1928	Harry Payne	(Woodford Green)	2:34.34	Windsor–Stamford Bridge
1929	Harry Payne	(Woodford Green)	2:30.58	Windsor–Stamford Bridge
1930	Dunky Wright	(Maryhill H)	2:38.30	Windsor–Stamford Bridge
1931	Dunky Wright	(Maryhill H)	2:49.55	Windsor–Stamford Bridge
1932	Donald McNab Robertson	(Maryhill H)	2:34.33	Windsor–White City
1933	Donald McNab Robertson	(Maryhill H)	2:43.14	Windsor–White City
1934	Donald McNab Robertson	(Maryhill H)	2:41.55	Windsor–White City
1935	Albert Norris	(Polytechnic H)	3:02.58	Windsor–White City
1936	Donald McNab Robertson	(Maryhill H)	2:35.03	Windsor–White City
1937	Donald McNab Robertson	(Maryhill H)	2:37.20	Windsor–White City
1938	Jack Beman	(Birchfield H)	2:36.40	Windsor–White City
1939	Donald McNab Robertson	(Maryhill H)	2:35.37	Windsor–White City
1946	Squire Yarrow	(Polytechnic H)	2:43.15	Windsor–White City
1947	Jack Holden	(Tipton H)	2:33.21	Loughborough
1948	Jack Holden	(Tipton H)	2:36.45	Windsor–Chiswick
1949	Jack Holden	(Tipton H)	2:34.11	Birmingham
1950	Jack Holden	(Tipton H)	2:31.04	Reading
1951	Jim Peters	(Essex Beagles)	2:31.42	Birmingham
1952	Jim Peters	(Essex Beagles)	2:20.43	Windsor–Chiswick
1953	Jim Peters	(Essex Beagles)	2:22.29	Cardiff
1954	Jim Peters	(Essex Beagles)	2:17.40	Windsor–Chiswick
1955	Robert McMinnis	(Sutton H)	2:39.35	Reading
1956	Harry Hicks	(Hampstead H)	2:26.15	Port Sunlight
1957	Eddie Kirkup	(Rotherham H)	2:22.28	Watford
1958	Colin Kemball	(Wolverhampton)	2:22.28	Windsor–Chiswick

AAA Marathon Champions contd.

Year	Name	Club	Time	Location
1959	Christopher Fleming-Smith	(Rotherham)	2:30.11	Watford
1960	Brian Kilby	(Coventry Godiva)	2:22.45	Welwyn Garden City
1961	Brian Kilby	(Coventry Godiva)	2:24.37	Enfield
1962	Brian Kilby	(Coventry Godiva)	2:26.15	Welwyn Garden City
1963	Brian Kilby	(Coventry Godiva)	2:16.45	Coventry
1964	Brian Kilby	(Coventry Godiva)	2:23.01	Coventry
1965	Bill Adcocks	(Coventry Godiva)	2:16.50	Port Talbot
1966	Graham Taylor	(Cambridge H)	2:19.04	Windsor–Chiswick
1967	Jim Alder	(Morpeth H)	2:16.08	Baddesley
1968	Tim Johnston	(Portsmouth AC)	2:15.26	Cwmbran
1969	Ron Hill	(Bolton Utd H)	2:13.42	Manchester
1970	Don Faircloth	(Croydon H)	2:18.15	Windsor–Chiswick
1971	Ron Hill	(Bolton Utd H)	2:12.39	Manchester
1972	Lutz Philipp	(West Germany)	2:12.50	Manchester
1973	Ian Thompson	(Luton Utd)	2:12.40	Harlow
1974	Akio Usami	(Japan)	2:15.16	Windsor
1975	Jeff Norman	(Altrincham)	2:15.50	Stoke
1976	Barry Watson	(Cambridge H)	2:15.08	Rotherham
1977	Dave Cannon	(Gateshead H)	2:15.02	Rugby
1978	Tony Simmons	(Luton Utd)	2:12.33	Sandbach
1979	Greg Hannon	(Duncairn)	2:13.06	Coventry
1980	Ian Thompson	(Luton Utd)	2:14.00	Milton Keynes
1981	Hugh Jones	(Ranelagh H)	2:14.07	Rugby
1982	Steve Kenyon	(Salford H)	2:11.40	Gateshead
1983	Mike Gratton	(Invicta AC)	2:09.43	London

Women's AAA Marathon Champions

Year	Name	Club	Time	Location
1978	Margaret Lockley	(Luton Utd)	2:55.08	Ryde
1979	Joyce Smith	(Barnet L)	2:41.37	Sandbach

Women's AAA Marathon Champions contd.

1980	Joyce Smith	(Barnet L)	2:41.22	London
1981	Leslie Watson	(London Olympiades)	2:49.08	Rugby
1982	Kathryn Binns	(Sale H)	2:36.12	Windsor
1983	Glynis Penny	(Cambridge H)	2:36.21	London

Polytechnic Marathon

1909	Fred Barrett	(Polytechnic H)	2:42.31	Windsor–Stamford Bridge
1910	No race owing to death of the King			(via Uxbridge and Hanwell)
1911	Henry Green	(Herne Hill H)	2:46.39	
1912	James Corkey	(Canada)	2:36.56	
1913	Alexis Ahlgren	(Sweden)	2:36.07	
1914	Ahmed Djebelia	(France)	2:46.31	
1919	E. Woolston	(Machine Gun Corps)	2:52.31	
1920	Arthur Mills	(Leicester H)	2:37.41	
1921	Arthur Mills	(Leicester H)	2:51.42	
1922	Arthur Mills	(Leicester H)	2:47.31	
1923	Aksel Jensen	(Denmark)	2:40.47	
1924	Dunky Wright	(Scotland)	2:53.18	
1925	Sam Ferris	(RAF)	2:35.59	
1926	Sam Ferris	(RAF)	2:42.25	
1927	Sam Ferris	(RAF)	2:40.33	
1928	Sam Ferris	(RAF)	2:41.03	
1929	Sam Ferris	(RAF)	2:40.48	
1930	Stanley Smith	(Birchfield H)	2:42.24	
1931	Sam Ferris	(RAF)	2:41.55	
1932	Sam Ferris	(RAF)	2:35.31	
1933	Sam Ferris	(RAF)	2:36.33	Windsor–White City
1934	Dunky Wright	(Scotland)	2:56.30	(via Datchet, Western Avenue)

Polytechnic Marathon contd.

Year	Name	Club	Time	Course
1935	Albert Norris	(Polytechnic H)	2:48.38	
1936	Albert Norris	(Polytechnic H)	2:35.20	
1937	Albert Norris	(Polytechnic H)	2:48.40	
1938	Henry Palme	(Sweden)	2:42.00	Windsor–Chiswick
1939	Henry Palme	(Sweden)	2:36.56	
1940	Leslie Griffiths	(Herne Hill H)	2:53.42	Wartime Course No.1–Windsor
1941	George Humphreys	(Woodford Green)	3:12.36	Wartime Course No.2–Local roads in Chiswick
1942	Leslie Griffiths	(Reading AC)	2:53.57	
1943	Leslie Griffiths	(Reading AC)	2:53.14	
1944	Tom Richards	(Mitcham AC)	2:56.40	
1945	Tom Richards	(Mitcham AC)	2:48.45	
1946	Horace Oliver	(Reading AC)	2:38.12	Windsor–Chiswick
1947	Cecil Ballard	(Surrey AC)	2:36.53	
1948	Jack Holden	(Tipton H)	2:36.45	
1949	Jack Holden	(Tipton H)	2:42.52	
1950	Jack Holden	(Tipton H)	2:33.07	
1951	Jim Peters	(Essex Beagles)	2:29.28	
1952	Jim Peters	(Essex Beagles)	2:20.43	
1953	Jim Peters	(Essex Beagles)	2:18.41	
1954	Jim Peters	(Essex Beagles)	2:17.40	
1955	Robert McMinnis	(RAF)	2:36.23	
1956	Ron Clarke	(Herne Hill H)	2:20.16	
1957	Eddie Kirkup	(Rotherham)	2:27.05	
1958	Colin Kemball	(Wolverhampton)	2:22.28	

Polytechnic Marathon contd.

Year	Winner	Club	Time	Notes
1959	Dennis O'Gorman	(St Albans City)	2:25.12	
1960	Arthur Keily	(Derby & County)	2:19.06	
1961	Peter Wilkinson	(Derby & County)	2:20.25	
1962	Ron Hill	(Bolton Utd H)	2:20.59	
1963	Buddy Edelen	(Hadleigh Olympiads)	2:14.26	
1964	Basil Heatley	(Coventry Godiva)	2:13.55	
1965	Morio Shigematsu	(Japan)	2:12.00	
1966	Graham Taylor	(Cambridge H)	2:19.04	
1967	Fergus Murray	(Oxford Univ)	2:19.06	
1968	Kenji Kimihara	(Japan)	2:15.15	
1969	Phil Hampton	(Royal Navy AC)	2:25.22	
1970	Don Faircloth	(Croydon H)	2:18.15	
1971	Phil Hampton	(Royal Navy AC)	2:18.31	
1972	Don Faircloth	(Croydon H)	2:31.52*	Windsor–Chiswick, but 29 miles by error
1973	Bob Sercombe	(Newport H)	2:19.48	Under distance; Windsor
1974	Akio Usami	(Japan)	2:15.16	Windsor
1975	No race			
1976	Bernie Plain	(Cardiff AAC)	2:15.43	
1977	Ian Thompson	(Luton Utd)	2:14.32	
1978	Dave Francis	(Westbury H)	2:19.05	
1979	Mike Gratton	(Invicta AC)	2:19.53	
1980	Tony Byrne	(Salford H)	2:22.28	
1981	Bernie Plain	(Cardiff AAC)	2:24.07	
1982	Graham Ellis	(Holmfirth H)	2:23.28	
1983	Alan McGee	(Southampton & Eastleigh AC)	2:22.55	

Polytechnic Marathon – Women's Section

1978	Gillian Adams	(Aldershot)	2:54.11
1979	Jane Davies	(Epsom/Ewell H)	3:21.23
1980	Gillian Adams	(Aldershot)	2:45.11
1981	Caroline Rodgers	(Highgate H)	2:51.03
1982	Kathryn Binns	(Sale H)	2:36.12
1983	Val Howe	(Bracknell AC)	3:05.40

London Marathon

1981	Eq. Dick Beardsley	(USA)	2:11.48
	Inge Simonsen	(Norway)	
1982	Hugh Jones	(Ranelagh H)	2:09.24
1983	Mike Gratton	(Invicta AC)	2:09.43

London Marathon – Women's Section

1981	Joyce Smith	(Barnet Ladies)	2:29.57
1982	Joyce Smith	(Barnet Ladies)	2:29.43
1983	Grete Waitz	(Norway)	2:25.29

Boston Marathon

24 miles 1232 yards

1897	John J. McDermott	(USA)	2:55.10
1898	Ronald J. McDonald	(USA)	2:42.00
1899	Lawrence J. Brignolia	(USA)	2:54.38
1900	James J. Caffrey	(Canada)	2:39.45
1901	James J. Caffrey	(Canada)	2:29.24
1902	Samuel A. Mellor, Jr	(USA)	2:43.12
1903	John C. Lorden	(USA)	2:41.30
1904	Michael Spring	(USA)	2:38.05
1905	Fred Lorz	(USA)	2:38.26

Boston Marathon contd.

1906	Timothy Ford	(USA)	2:45.45	
1907	Tom Longboat	(Canada)	2:24.24	
1908	Thomas P. Morrissey	(USA)	2:25.44	
1909	Henri Renaud	(USA)	2:53.37	
1910	Frederick Cameron	(Canada)	2:28.53	
1911	Clarence DeMar	(USA)	2:21.40	
1912	Michael Ryan	(USA)	2:21.19	
1913	Fritz Carlson	(USA)	2:25.15	
1914	James Duffy	(Canada)	2:25.02	
1915	Edouard Fabre	(Canada)	2:31.42	
1916	Arthur V. Roth	(USA)	2:27.17	
1917	William Kennedy	(USA)	2:28.38	
1918	Not held			
1919	Carl Linder	(USA)	2:29.14	
1920	Peter Trivoulidas	(USA)	2:29.31	
1921	Frank Zuna	(USA)	2:18.58	
1922	Clarence DeMar	(USA)	2:18.10	
1923	Clarence DeMar	(USA)	2:23.38	
1924	Clarence DeMar	(USA)	2:29.41	26 miles 209 yards
1925	Charles Mellor	(USA)	2:33.01	
1926	John Miles	(Canada)	2:25.41	
1927	Clarence DeMar	(USA)	2:40.23	26 miles 385 yards
1928	Clarence DeMar	(USA)	2:37.08	
1929	John Miles	(Canada)	2:33.09	
1930	Clarence DeMar	(USA)	2:34.49	
1931	James Henigan	(USA)	2:46.46	

Boston Marathon contd.

Year	Name	Country	Time	Distance
1932	Paul de Bruyn	(Germany)	2:33.37	
1933	Leslie Pawson	(USA)	2:31.02	
1934	David Komonen	(Canada)	2:32.54	
1935	John A. Kelley	(USA)	2:32.08	
1936	Ellison Brown	(USA)	2:33.41	
1937	Walter Young	(Canada)	2:33.20	
1938	Leslie Pawson	(USA)	2:35.35	
1939	Ellison Brown	(USA)	2:28.52	
1940	Gerard Cote	(Canada)	2:38.29	
1941	Leslie Pawson	(USA)	2:30.38	
1942	Bernard Smith	(USA)	2:26.52	
1943	Gerard Cote	(Canada)	2:28.26	
1944	Gerard Cote	(Canada)	2:31.51	
1945	John A. Kelley	(USA)	2:30.41	
1946	Stylianos Kyriakidis	(Greece)	2:29.27	
1947	Jun Bok Suh	(Korea)	2:25.39	
1948	Gerard Cote	(Canada)	2:31.02	
1949	Karl Gosta Leandersson	(Sweden)	2:31.51	
1950	Kee Yong Ham	(Korea)	2:32.39	
1951	Shigeki Tanaka	(Japan)	2:27.45	
1952	Doroteo Flores	(Guatemala)	2:31.53	
1953	Keizo Yamada	(Japan)	2:18.51	25 miles 938 yards
1954	Veikko Karvonen	(Finland)	2:20.39	
1955	Hideo Hamamura	(Japan)	2:18.22	
1956	Antti Viskari	(Finland)	2:14.14	
1957	John J. Kelley	(USA)	2:20.05	26 miles 385 yards

Boston Marathon contd.

1958	Franjo Mihalic	(Yugoslavia)	2:25.54
1959	Eino Oksanen	(Finland)	2:22.42
1960	Paavo Kotila	(Finland)	2:20.54
1961	Eino Oksanen	(Finland)	2:23.39
1962	Eino Oksanen	(Finland)	2:23.48
1963	Aurele Vandendriessche	(Belgium)	2:18.58
1964	Aurele Vandendriessche	(Belgium)	2:19.59
1965	Morio Shigematsu	(Japan)	2:16.33
1966	Kenji Kimihara	(Japan)	2:17.11
1967	Dave McKenzie	(New Zealand)	2:15.45
1968	Amby Burfoot	(USA)	2:22.17
1969	Yoshiaki Unetani	(Japan)	2:13.49
1970	Ron Hill	(Great Britain)	2:10.30
1971	Alvaro Mejia	(Colombia)	2:18.45
1972	Olavi Suomalainen	(Finland)	2:15.39
1973	Jon Anderson	(USA)	2:16.03
1974	Neil Cusack	(Eire)	2:13.39
1975	Bill Rodgers	(USA)	2:09.55
1976	Jack Fultz	(USA)	2:20.19
1977	Jermoe Drayton	(Canada)	2:14.46
1978	Bill Rodgers	(USA)	2:10.13
1979	Bill Rodgers	(USA)	2:09.27
1980	Bill Rodgers	(USA)	2:12.11
1981	Toshihiko Seko	(Japan)	2:09.26
1982	Alberto Salazar	(USA)	2:08.51
1983	Greg Meyer	(USA)	2:09.01

Boston Marathon – Women's Section

1972	Nina Kuscsik	(USA)	3:10.26
1973	Jackie Hansen	(USA)	3:05.59
1974	Miki Gorman	(USA)	2:47.11
1975	Liane Winter	(West Germany)	2:42.24
1976	Kim Merritt	(USA)	2:47.10
1977	Miki Gorman	(USA)	2:48.33
1978	Gayle Barron	(USA)	2:44.52
1979	Joan Benoit	(USA)	2:35.15
1980	Jacqueline Gareau	(Canada)	2:34.28
1981	Allison Roe	(New Zealand)	2:26.45
1982	Charlotte Teske	(West Germany)	2:29.33
1983	Joan Benoit	(USA)	2:22.43

New York City Marathon

1970	Garry Muhrcke	(Millrose AA)	2:31.39
1971	Norm Higgins	(Age Group AA)	2:22.55
1972	Sheldon Karlin	(College Park, Md)	2:27.53
1973	Tom Fleming	(New York AC)	2:21.55
1974	Norbert Sander	(Millrose AA)	2:26.31
1975	Tom Fleming	(New York AC)	2:19.27
1976	Bill Rodgers	(Gtr Boston TC)	2:10.10
1977	Bill Rodgers	(Gtr Boston TC)	2:11.29
1978	Bill Rodgers	(Gtr Boston TC)	2:12.12
1979	Bill Rodgers	(Gtr Boston TC)	2:11.42
1980	Alberto Salazar	(Univ of Oregon)	2:09.41
1981	Alberto Salazar	(Athletics West)	2:08.13
1982	Alberto Salazar	(Athletics West)	2:09.29
1983	Rod Dixon	(New Zealand)	2:08.59

New York City Marathon — Women's Section

Year	Name	Club/Country	Time
1971	Beth Bonner	(New Jersey Chargers)	2:55.22
1972	Nina Kuscsik	(Suffolk AC)	3:18.42
1973	Nina Kuscsik	(Suffolk AC)	2:57.08
1974	Kathrine Switzer	(CPTC)	3:07.29
1975	Kim Merritt	(Parkside AC)	2:46.15
1976	Miki Gorman	(San Fernando Valley)	2:39.11
1977	Miki Gorman	(San Fernando Valley)	2:43.10
1978	Grete Waitz	(Norway)	2:32.30
1979	Grete Waitz	(Norway)	2:27.33
1980	Grete Waitz	(Norway)	2:25.42
1981	Allison Roe	(New Zealand)	2:25.29
1982	Grete Waitz	(Norway)	2:27.14
1983	Grete Waitz	(Norway)	2:27.00

Appendix II

IAAF Rules and Course Measurement

Extract from International Amateur Athletic Federation Rules:
Rule 165
Marathon Race
(42,195 m – 26 miles 385 yards)

1. The Marathon race shall be run on made-up roads; when traffic or similar circumstances make it unsuitable, the course, duly marked, may be on a bicycle path or footpath alongside the road, but not on soft ground such as grass verges or the like. The start and finish may be within an athletic arena.

Note: It is desirable to have a course with a single turning point, or, alternatively, a single circuit.

2. A competitor must retire at once from the race if ordered to do so by a member of the medical staff officially appointed and clearly identified by an armband.

3. The distance in kilometres and miles on the route shall be displayed to all competitors.

4. Refreshments shall be provided by the Organizers of the Race at approximately 5 km and thereafter at approximately every 5 km.

In addition, the organizers shall provide sponging points where water only shall be supplied, midway between two refreshment stations. Refreshments, which may either be provided by the organizer or by the athlete himself, shall be available at the stations nominated by the competitor. The refreshments shall be placed in such a manner that they are easily accessible for the competitors or so that they may be put into the hands of the competitors. A competitor taking refreshments at a place other than the refreshment points appointed by the organizers renders himself liable to disqualification.

5. The organizers of the Marathon Race must take care to ensure the safety of competitors. In the case of Olympic Games and Area or Group Championships or Games, the organizers must, where possible, give an assurance that the roads to be used for the Marathon will be closed in both directions i.e. not open to motorized traffic.

Rule 145
Measurements and Weights (extract)

5. In events over roads, the course shall be measured along the ideal line of running, i.e. the shortest possible path, in that section of the road permitted for the runners. The course must not measure less than the official distance for the event (i.e. for Marathon race 42,195 metres) and the variation in the measurement must not exceed 50 metres in all meetings under Rule 12 (*major Games and championships*), i.e. a Marathon course must be between 42,195 and 42,245 metres.

IAAF Notes on the Measurement of Road Courses

1. It is important that the distance of a race on roads should be measured as accurately as possible, and that the measurement should be checked.

2. *Where to take measurements:*
Whatever method of measurement is employed, the course should be measured one metre from the verge of the road and in the direction of running or walking; but where a competitor would not keep to this position, for example, along a zig-zag road, the course should be measured along the path which the competitor would be likely to take, but without anywhere crossing the crown of the road.

3.(i) *Methods of measuring not recommended:*
Motor vehicle mileage recorders, cyclometers and pedometers should *NOT* be used to measure road courses. Commercially available 'Fifth Wheels' and other similar devices should not be used unless calibrated along 'standard distances' as defined below.

The use of a surveyor's wheel is likewise not recommended; but if its use is unavoidable, it must be checked along a standard distance on the road, the 'error' thus determined and the appropriate allowance made when the course is measured. The operator should push the wheel at a speed not exceeding 3 miles or 5 kilometres an hour.

(ii) *A useful preparatory step:*
Attention is drawn to the use of maps of 1:25000 or larger scale in the planning of a course, before measurements on the road are made. This can save considerable time.

4. *Recommended method:*
When the course cannot be measured by a surveyor's steel tape, as will be generally the case, the method recommended is measurement by *calibrated cycle wheel*.

5. *Equipment needed:*
The equipment needed is an ordinary bicycle fitted with a *revolution counter* (as distinct from a cyclometer) which records every revolution of the front wheel, or records continuously as the wheel rotates. The revolution counter (which is similar in size to an ordinary cyclometer) is mounted on the front hub. The mounting depends on the model used.

6. *Procedure to follow:*
The cycle is ridden over the road course and the number of revolutions of the front wheel recorded. Immediately before, and again, if possible, immediately after riding over the course, in order to check the tyre calibration, the cycle is ridden over an accurately known distance (called the 'standard distance') and the number of revolutions again determined.

   The length of the course is then calculated by simple arithmetic. The 'standard distance' must not be less than one kilometre (1093 yds), and should be measured and checked with a 50 ft or 100 ft (15 m or 30 m) surveyor's steel tape along a road of good surface, and preferably straight.

Alternatively, the 'standard distance' may be measured along a straight and reasonably level road by an Electronic Distance Meter. (Note: This is a modern surveying instrument for measuring distances, used for example in motorway construction.)

7. *Procedure for calibration:*
The exact procedure of calibration depends on whether the revolution counter is actuated by a striker on a spoke of the front wheel, thus recording once every revolution of the wheel, or whether the counter records continuously as the wheel rotates.

(i) *The method of calibration recording once for every revolution of the wheel is as follows:*
The hub of the front wheel of the cycle is lined up with the mark denoting the start of the 'standard distance'. The wheel is then lifted off the ground and rotated by hand until the counter-striker, mounted on a spoke, has just passed the striking position. The reading of the counter is then taken and the wheel lowered to the ground.

The spoke which lies between the front forks of the cycle is marked for easy identification (by means of a piece of tape near to the rim). When the counter again registers the wheel will have made exactly one revolution from the starting mark, and the marked spoke will have returned to the previous position between the forks.

The standard distance is ridden along, and the hub of the front wheel lined up with the mark at the end of the distance. The counter reading is again taken and the number of complete revolutions made, obtained by subtraction. Fractions of a revolution are measured by counting the number of spokes by which the marked spoke has passed beyond the fork. Thus, if there are 32 spokes in the wheel, fractions are measured in 32nd parts of a revolution.

The standard distance should be ridden over at least twice; the difference between the number of revolutions recorded on each occasion should not exceed one-eighth revolution.

(ii) If the counter records continuously as the wheel rotates it is only necessary to take the reading before and after riding the standard distance.

8. The calibration is valid for one measuring occasion only. Measurements should not be made when there are large variations in temperature, since a hot sun will expand the tyre. The cycle tyre should be in good condition and pumped up hard. A riding speed of about 16 km/hr (10–12 mph) is desirable. No part of the course should be walked.

9. The length of the course is calculated as follows:

Suppose 493 16/32 revolutions are recorded in riding the standard distance of 1,000 m, and 5582 revolutions are recorded in riding the course:

The length of the course will be $\dfrac{1000 \text{ m} \times 5582}{493.5} = 11311 \text{ m}$

This method of measurement is capable of determining the length of a road course with an error not exceeding 0.6 m per kilometre (1 yard per mile).